NOV – – 2003

D0583083

WITHDRAWN

Strategies of the Nation's Top Turkey Hunters

Strategies of the Nation's Top Turkey Hunters

*Expert Advice to Help You
Get a Gobbler This Season*

By the Editors of The Lyons Press

The Lyons Press
Guilford, Connecticut
An Imprint of The Globe Pequot Press

The Lyons Press in an imprint of The Globe Pequot Press.

10 9 8 7 6 5 4 3 2 1

Printed in the United States of America

Designed by Compset, Inc.

ISBN 1-59228-012-9

Library of Congress Cataloging-in-Publication Data is available
on file.

Acknowledgments

The Lyons Press would like to thank Editorial Director Jay Cassell and Assistant Editor Holly Rubino for their hard work in assembling this collection of thought-provoking and instructive turkey tales.

Contents

Introduction

What is it about turkey hunting that is so infectious? Why have so many millions of hunters become so obsessed with it? Why do so many people refer to turkeys as "big game," while every other bird is a "gamebird"? What is it with this bird?

To answer those questions, I can only look to myself, and to determine why I personally am now a card-carrying member of the turkey hunting legions. The answer, somehow, might be found in an episode that happened to me last May . . .

I have a cabin deep in New York's Catskill Mountains, right near the Beaverkill. In May, my idea of a perfect day is to be at my cabin, get up early in the morning, hunt turkeys until noon (end of legal hunting time in New York), have lunch and a nap, then go down the mountain and fish the Beaverkill for trout.

This particular weekend, I had driven up to the cabin late Friday night, grabbed a quick meal at the Roscoe Diner, and then driven up the four-wheel-drive road to my cabin. Quickly throwing some wood in the woodstove (the temperature was around 30 degrees F), I set the alarm for 4:15 A.M. and dove into my bed. The time was around 11:00 P.M.

When the alarm went off, I jolted awake, wondering where I was—I easily have the loudest wind-up alarm clock known to man—but I quickly figured it out. Downing a quick cup of instant coffee, throwing on my camo clothes, loading up my

12-gauge with No. 5 turkey loads . . . I was out the door. The sun wasn't even thinking about coming up yet.

There's a small green field about a mile from my cabin, and I headed in that direction. I had talked with a gobbler there the previous weekend, but the wind was so intense that I couldn't hear if he was coming in to my calls or not. I had eventually given up and gone back to bed.

This morning was different. Slight breeze, but pretty still, temperature in the high 30s, predicted to get into the 50s. This was a perfect time to be out in the turkey woods.

As I headed down the road, I could see the faint glimmer of the sun beginning to edge up toward the horizon. I called a few times with my slate call as I walked, as I have worked birds from the dirt road before. This time, nothing. I wanted to get to the green field quickly and set up, though, so I didn't waste much time calling. I just knew that bird was going to be in or near that field, and I wanted to get there in a hurry. He might even be the bird that outsmarted me last season, coming in quickly, gobbling within 50 yards of the field—I even saw his fan at that distance—just a bit too far away for a shot—and then heading up over the ridge and out of sight, for Lord knows what reason.

I got to the field by 5:00 A.M., eased into the woods, and listened. I'm one of those hunters who likes to just edge quietly into an area and listen—I don't think calling right away serves any purpose, to be honest. So I stood there and listened. And there, in the distance, I heard a faint gobble—maybe 300 yards away, although it was tough to tell.

Moving quickly, I closed the distance by 100 yards, then set up in a blowdown above a hemlock grove. I suspected he was in there, somewhere, roosted. I heard him again.

Pulling out my slate call, I made a few tree yelps, and got an immediate response. Now for the fun part. Yelping a few more times, I took out a wing flapper, flapped it half a dozen times, then started rustling the leaves, imitating hens coming down from the roost. I yelped a few more times, and now the bird was gobbling at my every sound . . . and, I realized, getting closer.

This calling duel went on for the next half hour at least. I'd call, he'd respond—back and forth, back and forth, with him all the while getting closer and closer. Soon I could tell he was within maybe 75 yards—his booming gobble shattering the morning silence time and again. I eased my gun up on my knee, put a diaphragm call in my mouth in case he got so close that I couldn't move my hands and use my slate call, and called again. He was just over the rise, I was certain, gobbling his fool head off. And I couldn't see him, and I couldn't get him to come any closer. Another twenty minutes went by. My frustrations mounted. Maybe I should move—even though he was hot, and gobbling like crazy, he was hung up, and obviously expecting me, the hen, to come to him.

I knew if I moved, he might see me. But if he heard me yelping and clucking from a different location, he might think I was leaving, and come rushing in. I decided I had to move—just 15 yards away. Getting up, hunching over, I ran to a large tree, slammed into the ground, quickly set up, and called again. Nothing. Silence. I called again. Silence. Maybe he was sneaking in quietly, so I shut up. Nothing. I called again. Silence.

He was gone. Had I heard another hen in the distance? I wasn't sure. But I had lost this little battle. It was 8:00 A.M.! I tried some other spots on the mountain that morning, but heard nothing. Then I went and had my nap, and went fishing.

That duel up on the mountain has bothered me ever since. How could I be so stupid? How could I screw up so royally? I've hunted turkeys for a long time—I should know better. I shouldn't have moved . . . or should I?

That's the enticement of turkey hunting, right there. It's like playing chess. You make a move, the bird makes a move. Sooner or later, somebody is going to get checkmate and win. It's usually the gobbler, too—after all, you're playing on his board, he's got better eyesight than you, and he has all the moves. All you can hope is that your ersatz hen imitations are going to trick him, and make him think there is a sexy hen out there in the woods, by that tree, just pining away for him, waiting for him to show up.

I never heard that bird again, for the rest of the season. Never heard *any* good gobbler again for the rest of the season, for that matter. But you'll never guess where I'm going to be come this May. Yup, I'll be at that green field, listening for a gobbler who has now fooled me two years in a row. This year, I don't care how smart he has become; he's mine! Why? Because I've added some more ammo to my turkey hunting arsenal— I've added this book!

Read it, and you'll know what I mean. For in this book are chapters that deal with all sorts of turkey hunting problems, from true experts such as Rob Keck, Eddie Salter, Harold Knight and John Trout, Jr. Personally, I'm paying particular attention to the chapter by Kathy Etling, called "Patience is a (Turkey Hunting) Virtue," which starts on page 137.

As you read through this book, you'll find chapters that apply to a variety of hunting situations: how to scout for birds before the season; how to deal with quiet birds; how to use decoys; how to call effectively; and how to hunt birds in the fall, a fast-growing part of turkey hunting. You'll also find some chapters in here that deal with the mindset of turkey hunting, the charisma. Robert F. Jones's piece, "The New Spring Rite," in the beginning of this book, is just such a chapter, putting everything in perspective. "The Teachings of Don Pepé," by Thomas

McIntyre, even gives you a look at hunting south of the border.

So sit back and enjoy. Come this spring, you'll be more prepared than ever to take on what is easily the wiliest bird on earth—the wild turkey.

Jay Cassell
January 15, 2003

Strategies of the Nation's Top Turkey Hunters

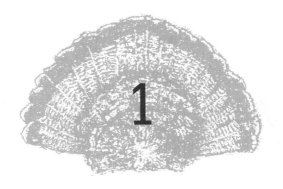

The New Spring Rite

*How to Find, Entice, Take, and Prepare
America's Premier Gamebird*

By Robert F. Jones

*Robert F. Jones was the author of several highly acclaimed
novels, including* The Run to Gitche Gumee; *five works of
nonfiction, including* Dancers in the Sunset Sky, *a collec-
tion of sporting essays; and the editor of the anthology* On
Killing. *His work appeared in* Sports Afield, Men's Journal,
Outdoor Life, Big Sky Journal, Audubon, Time, Sports
Ilustrated, Life, People, Harper's, *and* The New York
Times. *He lived in West Rupert, Vermont.*

In the early days of this republic, the North American wild
turkey ranged in greater or lesser numbers over three quarters of the nation and well down into Mexico. So tasty was
the bird that Benjamin Franklin—statesman and trencherman

1

extraordinaire—nominated it on culinary grounds alone as our national bird. But by the beginning of this century, thanks to market gunning and ruinous logging, turkeys were nearly extinct. On the eve of World War II, only about thirty thousand remained, most of them in the South and Southwest.

For a while, state wildlife agencies, with the help of local rod and gun clubs, tried restocking with pen-raised birds, but it didn't work. These half-tame turkeys were happier in barnyards than in the big woods, fell easy prey to predators, and died in droves during hard winters. Not until the development of the cannon-propelled capture net in the 1960s did game managers have a tool for livetrapping mature wild turkeys and planting them in suitable habitat elsewhere. The slow return of Eastern-turkey farmlands to second-growth forest enhanced the process. In Vermont, an initial transplant in 1968 of thirty-one birds from New York State thrived so well that a spring gobbler season was opened five years later. The rest of New England, from Maine to Connecticut, was restocked over the next few years, while similar restoration programs were succeeding all across the country.

Today, huntable populations of America's premier game-bird exist in every state but Alaska (the total is about two million). You can even hunt them in Hawaii. The return of the wild turkey is one of the greatest wildlife success stories of the twentieth century.

What's more, turkey hunting is good for our souls. It's just about the most politically correct thing you can do in today's gender-sensitive America. In fact, it beats mountain biking, whitewater rafting, in-line skating and even fly fishing as "with it" sports for the twenty-first century. How can this be? Simple. More than any other outdoor endeavor you can name, the pursuit of wild spring gobblers brings out a man's feminine side.

A trophy gobbler: the reason for doing it. (Credit: John Trout, Jr.)

First we put on makeup and/or a veil, dress up in a cunning new outfit carefully chosen to match the colors of our surroundings. Then we go out in the spring woods, warblers trilling all around us, in hopes of a torrid assignation. We pose seductively against a tree and commence to work our girlish wiles. Clucks and whines, whistles and purrs, yelps and cutts. *Come on, Big Guy, I'm yours for the taking.*

Rule Number One: Find the Birds

Scouting is the single most important ingredient to success in hunting the North American wild turkey. It's even more important—though barely—than knowing how to talk turkey. You have to know where those birds are roosting if you're going to get a shot at one next morning.

Just walking through the woods hoping to spot a gobbler won't do it. A turkey can see or hear you long before you'll be aware of his presence. Going into the woods before dawn, then sitting and listening for tree yelps or wake-up gobbles won't do it either, unless you're lucky enough to have set up by chance near a roosting tree. Unless you can stalk as silently and unobtrusively as a house cat, the moment you begin to move in on a distant gobbler, the odds against your success rise ruinously.

Your best bet is to "roost" the birds the evening before you hunt. Male turkeys will sound off with territorial gobbles when they bed down for the night, sometimes for twenty minutes or more. An hour at dusk spent walking or driving the dirt roads and trails of turkey country, and listening carefully every few hundred yards, will tell you if any gobblers are around. The sound is loud and unmistakable. To get a better fix on it you can answer the real gobble with one from your box, or hoot like an owl, caw like a crow, bark like dog, even slam your truck door. I've known gobblers to respond to all of those sounds.

Over much of their range, wild turkeys like to roost on the lower horizontal limbs of pine trees (white pines in my New England territory), so be sure to mark the clumps of pines from which you think those bedtime gobbles are coming. Next morning, well before first light, you should be in the woods (about 50 or 100 yards uphill from the suspected roosting tree), clad in camo, your calls at hand, set up with your back against a broad tree trunk and your gun ready to be raised with minimal movement.

As the gray light begins to filter through the trees, the first sounds you'll likely hear are tree yelps: soft, muffled squeaks that are the turkey's equivalent of the moans, groans and curses we (or at least I) make on awakening each morning. Then you'll hear sounds like a sheet or blanket being shaken—its wings flapping, the morning wake-up stretch—and you can imitate it by slapping your cap against your leg. The gobbler might mistake your noise for that of a hen flying down.

Next, the gobbler will start sounding off his territorial imperative. You can often provoke this clarion call with an owl hoot, but
don't overdo it. Old Longbeard has heard it all, and he didn't get
that big by being dumb. Compared to the earlier noises, his first
gobble will sound like a bugle call—right on top of you, if you've
marked the roost well. (An older, trophy-sized tom has a clear,
melodious gobble. Jakes, like teenagers, tend to have squeaky
voices.) Then, sometimes as much as half an hour later, you'll
hear the gobbler fly down, a sound I can liken only to that of your
spouse falling down the cellar stairs with a bucket of wet wash.

What Every Gobbler Wants

Early in the season, a gobbler won't be interested in breakfast.
What he wants is sex. He may already have a harem of hens
who've roosted near him, and will begin courting them the moment he hits the ground. This makes it tough for the hunter, because if you start to make seductive hen yelps, cuts and cackles
on your box or diaphragm call, the real hens will do their
damnedest to keep that gobbler from straying. I've known hens
to run up to me, where I sat clumsily imitating them, ready for a
fight, and I've seen others, more often than I care to remember,
purposely cut off and distract a gobbler who'd begun responding to my plaintive calls.

Later in the season, and sometimes later in the mornings
during the early season, the hens will wander off from the gobbler to feed or sit their nests, but the old patriarch will still be
horny. Your chances of deceiving him are better at these times,
and sometimes you'll get a gobbler and two or three jakes charging you all at once.

One morning a few years back, I was set up on a shoulder of
Shatterack Mountain, in southwestern Vermont, calling to a
gobbler at least a quarter mile across the hollow on the slopes
of Moffat Mountain to the east. I must have said something

right, because he suddenly began sprinting toward me, as fast as a running dog. Down he tore with two jakes hot on his trail, across a dirt road, and up toward where I was sitting. A little fold in the ground ahead of me obscured the gobbler for about a minute, but quicker than I could raise my shotgun he was on top of me, not five yards away. As he saw me raise the gun, he turned to split—but I hit him, hard in the neck, and he flopped. The jakes then came skidding to a halt atop the fold. One of them got airborne, flying right over my head. I centered him on the rise.

How to Throw a Hen Party

More often than not, you'll have to work your birds long and cunningly to lure them within shooting range. There are countless devices on the market for calling turkeys, from hinged-lid cedar boxes to slate-and-peg scratch calls; one-handed plunger calls to wingbone suction yelpers to mouth-held diaphragms. The Dunn's catalog alone lists seven full pages of turkey calls. Most of them come with instructional videos that will teach you turkey talk and how to use the calls best. For starters, though, the only calls you really have to master are the:

Cluck. One short syllable that varies in volume and sharpness depending on what the hen wishes to say (softer for reassurance, sharper for calling her brood to attention).

Yelp. Two syllables, the first one higher-pitched than the second. This call usually occurs in an evenly spaced series of two or three yelps.

Cutt. A series of choppy, high-pitched, rapid yelps used by the hen to excite a gobbler during the mating season. You can often call back an alarmed or disillusioned young gobbler with an insistent series of cutts.

Alarm putt. A series of very loud, sharp, and distinct clucks that sound, as a friend of mine says, like fingernails on a blackboard. I sometimes use this call, with a mouth diaphragm so my hands are free for the gun, at the last possible moment to bring the gobbler's head upright when he's fanned and strutting toward me. Then I sight quickly on his neck and shoot.

As you gain skill with your calls, you can experiment with other sounds, like the *kee-hee* run (a whistle or whine, three notes rising in pitch, made by young turkeys when they've been separated from their mother during the fall season), which is best imitated with a diaphragm call; or the *purr*, a reassuring, musical whirring or fluttering noise that you can perform by pursing your lips and making a sound like an outboard motor. It will sometimes bring a reluctant gobbler those last few steps into shooting range.

There are many variations possible within this simple avian language: subtle tones, little billings and cooings, a certain Stradivarius-like range possible, from raspy vibratos to silken siren-calls; all of which will come to you with a bit of practice. And there is absolutely no better place to practice them than in the spring turkey woods—whether they're the blooming dogwoods and shad-bush of New England or the blue-flagged palmetto swamps of south Florida; or among the wild crocuses of the Rockies or the myriad wildflowers of the Texas Hill Country. It's all turkey country now, and it's all quite splendid.

Use Enough Gun

Though many states, especially those in the West and Southwest, allow the use of rifles for turkeys, some modern variant of the old Pilgrim blunderbuss is still the best and most exciting way to hunt the birds. You have to get them in close for the shotgun—that's what the game is all about. To see a gobbler in full display, chest puffed and glinting as he struts; the great fan spread; that bald knob changing colors from red to blue to bone-white as rapidly as a neon sign; to hear him spitting and booming sweet nothings to what he thinks of as his prospective mate—and then to lure him even closer, within 25 yards at least—is a nerve-corroding experience rarely equaled in any other form of hunting. When you finally hit the trigger, it's almost an anticlimax.

But you'd better lay it on that gobbler accurately and hard, right then, with the right gun and the right load, or it all will have gone for naught. A mature turkey is tough; he can absorb a lot of shot, and then get up from what you thought was surely a knockout blow and run clear out of sight like a cheetah. Unless you do things right, the next news you'll have of him is from the crows circling over some far-off glade where he lays dead from your misplaced shot.

Gauge. A wild turkey is a big-game animal, and it's just plain criminal to shoot him with anything lighter than a 12-gauge. Sure, you can luck out and kill the odd bird with a 20-gauge (I've even heard of it being done with a .410) but that's show-off stuff. A friend of mine, Tim Joern of Whitefish, Montana, uses a 10-gauge, a hellacious weapon nicknamed "Big Bob," and doesn't feel he's overgunned. Nor do I.

Action. A big-bore, full-choked, short-barreled, matte-finished autoloader is your best choice for a turkey gun. If you're calling well and the birds are hot, sometimes more than one turkey will respond to your allure—a big gobbler and perhaps as many as two or three jakes, all coming on the run. The autoloader allows you as many as five shots, if it's legal in your state to take more than one turkey, and the noise of the action is masked by the explosion. Very few gunners this side of Steve McQueen in *The Getaway* can work a pump action fast enough to hide the clamor of a moving slide. Pumps are all well and good for waterfowl, where the tolling birds are out in the open with nowhere to go but up once you've fired. But turkeys not hit by your first shot can instantly reverse course and disappear

A hunter gets ready for the shot. (Credit: John Trout, Jr.)

back into heavy cover the moment they've located the source of that loud, ugly noise.

My second choice for a turkey gun, oddly enough, is an over-and-under 12-gauge Beretta, the gun I use with different choke tubes for pheasants, sage hens, ducks and geese. I screw extra-full choke tubes in, which are the tightest I've been able to find. The gun has two beads on the rib, which allows a fairly close sight picture. The advantage of the double-barrel over a pump is the silence between first and second shots. Ivory hunters in Africa preferred double-barreled rifles for that same reason. Rarely can an animal or bird at close range locate the source of your first shot simply by the bang. The sound of a working bolt or pump slide, though, is a dead giveaway.

Sights. The minimum gun sights you should use are the abovementioned twin beads. Most shotgun manufacturers now market specially designed turkey guns, short in the barrel, with sling swivels already attached (a real convenience), and—most important—mounted either with a low-power scope, an optical sight or buckhorn-and-bead iron sights. Some of the last have the rear of the front blade painted white or fluorescent-orange, and for good reason: A black bead does not show up against the dark outline of a wild turkey. And a gobbler, even when he's totally deluded by your calling and is strutting in full display, holds his head down on his vaulted breast. You want to shoot for his tucked-away neck, not over or below it. Make sure you can see your front sight against a dark background.

One way to get a strutting turkey to raise his vulnerable head and stretch out his neck is to give an alarm putt on your diaphragm or box call at the last moment, when he's within shooting range. Almost inevitably, he'll stretch to full height, if only for an instant. That's when you hit the trigger.

Load. I use as much lead and powder as I can—which means three-inch magnums—packing buffered No. 4 or No. 5 copper-plated shot. Buffered loads are packed with plastic dust that holds the shot charge together the full length of the barrel. The copper plating keeps the shot from deforming in the barrel, and makes for better penetration when it arrives on target.

Bart Jacob, who's hunted them all, tells me that before he hung up his shotgun in favor of the bow some eight years ago, he used to shoot two magnum loads of No. 4 shot up front, backed by a load of No. 2s for a finishing shot. With that kind of punch he could kill out to 40 yards, though he tried to get the birds within 20—and usually succeeded.

Don't End Up the Turkey

Turkey hunting can be hazardous. You're wearing camouflage, working close to birds in heavy cover, making sounds like another turkey, and probably shooting magnum 12-gauge loads of No. 4 or No. 5 shot, backed up by a load of No. 2s, any of which can kill a man stone dead at close range. Here are some things not to do in the turkey woods, if you value your hide and those of your fellow hunters.

1. Don't wear any clothing that is red, white or blue. These are the colors of the gobbler's head, their intensities varying with the state of excitement, and it is the head of the turkey that any other hunter will be shooting at. Some hunters, even seasoned veterans, get carried away by self-delusion. I read a story not long ago about a turkey hunter who was answering the call of nature. He had lowered his camo pants and assumed the position, when a nearby hunter saw the white flash of his underdrawers. The victim survived, but now answers to the name of "Half-Ass."

2.   Don't set up in the open. Not only can an approaching gobbler see you more easily out there, but your upper body, especially in low light, will resemble the size, shape and color of a turkey. Always set up with a tree trunk or boulder at your back. Don't rely on immobility to spare you: Believe me, you'll twitch or sway or move your arms, if only in working your call, and another gunner may well mistake you for the gobbler of his dreams.

3.   Don't stalk or shoot at turkey sounds. Most serious turkey hunters these days sound enough like the real thing to fool even the experts. In the crowded East particularly, any turkey-like sound you hear on opening day, from yelp to cutt to cluck to gobble, will likely be that of another hunter. Even owl hoots are suspect. Shortly after I moved to Vermont in 1979, two hunters just down the road from me stalked each other sonically for nearly an hour. It ended only when one had killed the other.

4.   Don't gobble, especially in heavily hunted areas like New England or the South. Sure, you can often draw in a horny gobbler by making sounds like a rival. But a gobble might draw the fire of some trigger-happy neophyte only too eager to take a "brush shot" and see what he's hit later. Out West you might get away with it, but you never know.

5.   Don't call while you're on the move. That's only asking to be bushwhacked. If you hear an authentic turkey call, set up quickly while covering your back, and only then attempt to establish a dialogue.

6.   Don't wave at any hunter until you're sure he recognizes you as human. He has probably heard something, possibly you, and thinks the moment is at hand for the triumphant conclusion of his season. If you wave, he might shoot. When I see another hunter, I start singing in a loud, clear voice. My tune of choice: "I Can't Get No Satisfaction."

7. Don't try to pick up a wounded turkey. Those spurs are sharp; those wings can slap you silly. A dying turkey can pound the crap out of you. Instead, step on its neck to immobilize it, then cut its throat. Don't try to shoot its head off while it's pinned: You might blow your foot away.

8. Don't carry your turkey out by the feet. The wings will flap, and another hunter might mistake it for a live bird. Instead, bring along a plastic garbage bag or better yet, a fluorescent-orange hunting vest in which to wrap it. Carry the bird by the neck so the wings hang naturally. A few years ago, a kid in a nearby town was leaving the woods at first light carrying his turkey over his back by the feet. Walking through an open field, he saw a party of hunters going in and waved to them. They turned, their eyes widened, and they let fly. They hit him in the face and neck, but he lived.

9. Above all, don't shoot at anything unless you're sure it's a turkey. Otherwise you might end up the turkey of the day in more ways than one.

Turkeys from Coast to Coast

Although there are seven subspecies of *Meleagris gallopavo* in North America, we'll concern ourselves here only with the meleagrids that inhabit the U.S., all of which talk the same language and behave similarly, with minor variations depending on habitat. They all have a 270-degree field of vision and can see about eight times as well as humans. Their hearing is much sharper than ours as well. None are easy prey.

M.g. gallopavo, the Mexican progenitor of all the world's domestic turkeys, is probably extinct in the wild—or so say the experts. Originally tamed by the Aztecs, they were shipped to Spain by Cortez's conquistadors in about 1520, and quickly spread through the rest of Europe, where they were lumped into the folk consciousness with guinea fowl from the Ottoman

Empire. As a result, both birds were known as *turkie fowles*. When the Pilgrims arrive in Massachusetts in 1621, they brought domestic turkeys with them, not realizing that tastier wild birds would be virtually free for the killing in the New World. Now we know, but it's a lot tougher today.

M.g. silvestris, the Eastern wild turkey, ranges from New England to the Mississippi/Missouri drainage down to about Orlando, Florida, and northern Oklahoma. It had the widest original range and is the largest and most adaptable of the subspecies, weighing up to 30 pounds. (Domesticated strains have been known to reach 70 pounds.) All wild turkeys are omnivorous but a Virginia study showed *M.g. silvestris* eating as many as 354 species of plants and insects. Still, given its druthers, this Eastern bird prefers hard mast—acorns, beechnuts, hickory and butternuts. It likes to roost on the long, horizontal lower branches of white pines. The tail tips are dark brown with iridescent brown-tipped rump coverts.

M.g. Osceola, the Florida turkey, generally weighs less than the Eastern but is taller, with longer legs—better suited for running through the wet palmetto hammocks it calls home. More streamlined than the Easterner, *M.g. Osceola* has a smaller head that sometimes makes it look like a great blue heron. It feeds on grasses and insects among the palmettos, and on scrub oak mast in drier country. Coloring is the same as the Eastern bird's. Any turkey taken south of Disneyworld is most likely *M.g. Osceola*. Bart Jacob, who wrote a fine book called *The Grand Spring Hunt* and has also bagged a U.S. Grand Slam (all four subspecies found within American borders), feels *M.g. Osceola* are the wiliest of American turkeys. "They're on their original range," he says, "and they've always been hunted hard."

M.g. intermedia, the Rio Grande turkey, is primarily a bird of southern Texas, though it ranges into Oklahoma and the northern Texas and southwestern Oklahoma panhandles, where it overlaps with the Eastern subspecies and with the Merriam's turkey. In my experience, the Rio Grande runs in flocks larger than any of the others—I was once almost trampled by a "herd" of at least two hundred on the YO Ranch in the Texas Hill Country. It ranges through open grasslands, searching out insects, plant life and the ubiquitous shin oak acorns. It will travel up to five miles to roost in a tree no taller than a man if nothing better is available. Identifying features: white tail tips and cinnamon rump coverts.

M.g. merriami, Merriam's turkey, is bigger than the Rio Grande turkey but about the same size as the Eastern. It loves the high country, ranging as many as 40 miles in a day or two up and down the Rockies through ponderosa pine and piñon country, where it feeds on pine nuts and acorns from Gambel oaks. Unlike Easterns, Merriam's tend to feed downhill from the roost, so it's best to set up below them. You'll have to scout hard to find one, but once you do it's a bit easier to fool than the more heavily hunted Eastern, Florida or Rio Grande bird. Brilliantly bronze-colored, the Merriam's has creamy white tail tips, white rump coverts, light gray-white secondaries and distinctive white wing patches.

M.g. mexicana, the Gould's turkey of the southwest U.S. border country (southern New Mexico and Arizona) and Mexico, hangs out at elevations of 4500 to 7500 feet, mainly in the Sierra Madre Occidental. Also called the Mexican turkey, the Gould's is the tallest turkey of the five subspecies found in this country. The bird was first described by and named after the English ornithologist and bird painter John Gould. Its preferred food is manzanita berries. Because the country it inhabits is steep, arid, hot and dusty—chaparral and small piñon pine and juniper forests—it is the most physically demanding of the subspecies to hunt. Coloring of the Gould's is similar to that of the Merriam's, with white feathers on its rump and outer-tail coverts.

After the Hunt

If you cook it right, a wild turkey is to a Perdue Butterball as *pâté de foie gras* is to chalk. The breast meat is sweet, nutty, juicy— the essence of wild meat. The legs are a bit tough, but they are so tasty that to discard them should be a crime punishable by a lifetime loss of license. Along with the carcass, they make a thick, dark, meaty soup so tempting that just a whiff can revive the dead—namely me, after a hard day of hunting. Here are a few basic recipes:

Roast Wild Turkey

1. Stuff a drawn, plucked bird with pecans and sliced wild apples—the "feral" apples that spring up in my Vermont turkey woods are often more flavorful than the libelously misnamed Delicious variety you buy in most stores.
2. Add giblets and some wild leeks or a quartered onion.
3. The fatty "breast sponge" that gives the wild turkey his pouter-pigeon look should provide adequate self-basting, but if in doubt lay a few strips of unsalted bacon over the breast for added moisture.
4. Rub butter or margarine onto the legs.
5. Cover the breast, legs and sides with a roomy tent of aluminum foil to further the moistening process. The bird should baste itself, but if you want to take the time—and enjoy the fragrance more intensely—you can baste it every half hour with melted butter and the juices that drip into the roasting pan.
6. Roast at 350°, 10 minutes per pound. Turn the oven down to 325° if the bird is getting too brown, *i.e.*, dry.

7. Remove the bacon and the foil tent for the last half hour or 45 minutes to allow the bird to brown properly and the skin to get crisp.

8. Serve with salad, wild rice or potatoes, and gravy made from the drippings. I like a little cold cranberry or wild elderberry jelly as a condiment. A chilled Merlot or white Zinfandel goes well alongside.

Hot Turkey Sandwiches

1. Slice the cooled meat of the thighs and breast about a ¼-inch thick and across the grain.

2. Fry it in a lightly oiled, preheated pan for a minute or two on each side. (Use your judgment here—you don't want meat the texture of leather.)

3. Heat up the leftover gravy, or make some fresh from the drippings in the pan.

4. Cut a few slices of home baked multigrain sourdough bread, or whatever, and toast them if you choose. Butter them lavishly. Pour gravy over the bread and turkey. Slice a dill pickle and lay it on the plate with some green onions and a hefty dollop of gravy.

5. Pop a beer—the best musical prelude to the feast that follows.

Turkey Soup with Wild Mushrooms

1. Cut up the carcass with game shears. Add the leg and wing-bones and dump it all into a pot.

2. Add chopped onions, garlic, celery, carrots, one bay leaf, a teaspoon of thyme, six peppercorns, two crushed juniper berries and some parsley.

3. Cover with water and/or chicken broth.

4. Bring it to a boil, then simmer until the meat begins to fall from the bones. Add liquid as needed.

5. Peel the meat from the bones and set it aside to cool—you can add the meat later, but if you cook it too long it becomes tasteless, though the soup will be enriched in the process. Return the bones to the soup pot.

6. When the soup thickens, replace the meat and add dried chanterelles or some other wild mushrooms.

Talk'n Turkey

By Rob Keck

Rob Keck is the CEO of the National Wild Turkey Federation. He has been a columnist and illustrator for Turkey Call *magazine and has lectured on turkey hunting and calling. Keck hosts two award-winning television programs: "Turkey Call" (TNN) and "Turkey Country" (Outdoor Channel).* Petersen's Hunting Magazine *has named him one of hunting's twenty-five most influential people in the twentieth century.*

When I first began hunting wild turkeys in my native hills of Pennsylvania forty years ago, the sport was made up of a dedicated legion of turkey hunters primarily focused on fall turkey hunting since that was the only season open there. Huntable populations of turkeys were scattered among the historic strongholds of North America where the destruction of forests and unregulated market hunting of the early 1900s had failed to wipe them out. Fortunately for my fellow Pennsylvanians and me, our state was one of those strongholds.

Rob Keck with an awe-inspiring gobbler. (Credit: NWTF)

Unfortunately, there was no national organization to bring us together, leaving much of our knowledge to be shared firsthand around the cracker barrels of country stores, at the occasional calling contests at small sportsmen's shows and in the hunting camps of our country's rural backwoods.

Then, in 1973, came the National Wild Turkey Federation, shaped by a group of hunters and biologists concerned about wild turkeys and interested in working with state and federal wildlife agencies to expand their populations. A number of states were already in the process of restoring or reestablishing viable populations within their borders and with the NWTF, the perfect vehicle to help these agencies garner additional funds and volunteer help was created. It was also the perfect way for turkey hunters to come together on a much broader scale, to share their ideas and hunting knowledge on everything from how to use or make certain calls to creating the best setups when working a tom. It filled a role of providing turkey hunting and calling know-how because of the generations that proceeded with no turkey experience.

Eager to play a role in this effort, I became involved with the newly-formed NWTF, where I soon went to work increasing the ranks of its chapters and membership; first as a volunteer helping form the Pennsylvania Chapter, then creating the first Grand National Calling Championships, writing a column for *Turkey Call* magazine and later being hired as its CEO, a post I've held since 1981. When the NWTF was first founded in 1973, there were an estimated 1.3 million wild turkeys and 1.5 million turkey hunters. Today, thanks to the work of the wildlife agencies and the Federation's partners and 450,000 volunteers, there are an estimated 5.6 million wild turkeys and 2.6 million turkey hunters.

I have seen a lot of changes in the turkey hunting world since those early days when the only choices in camouflage were old military fatigues and hunters used the same shotguns to hunt gobblers as they did ducks, rabbits and squirrels. With the growth of the sport has come a whole host of products geared especially for the turkey hunter, including an array of realistic camo patterns, specialty shotguns and turkey loads, an endless variety of calls, turkey hunting vests, decoys, seats, and other items.

While I'm proud of the influence the NWTF has had on the creation of many of these products and the work we've done to assist wildlife agencies in placing turkeys in suitable habitats, one of my great joys and sources of pride is sharing the hunting knowledge I and others have learned during our time afield with other hunters, particularly new ones. Through the Federation's publications and television programs, the organization has helped create hundreds of thousands of safe, woods wise hunters.

Following are a dozen of my favorite tips which offer an assortment of information to carry you from pre-season planning to a lifetime of successful turkey seasons.

Mapping Your Way

Having intimate knowledge of the land you plan to hunt is key to a successful and enjoyable spring or fall.

Prior to traversing new countryside, it's important to study topographic, property and roadway features by reviewing aerial photographs and maps of the terrain. This can be important as a river, fence, or even downed trees can interrupt a gobbler's approach to your calls enough to turn your hunt from one of success to one where you leave the woods empty-handed. Maps can detail these physical features like rivers, roads, canyons, mountains, swamps and property lines, which all play a role in the outcome of your hunt. Understanding these features before your next trek to new country makes you a knowledgeable hunter and can help you best decide where to set up when working a gobbling tom.

Sources of maps include:

Topographic: U.S. Geological Survey, Map Distribution Federal Center, Building 41, Box 25286, Denver, Colorado 80225.

Aerial Photographs: Check your local office of the Soil Conservation Service or your county tax office.

Other maps: Check your state wildlife agency, USDA Forest Service, Bureau of Land Management or check the Yellow Pages under "Maps."

Taking Aim

Miss a turkey with a shotgun?

"No way!" you say.

Well, you may have taken limits of ducks and geese with your ol' scattergun, but a 20-pound standing gobbler is still never a sure thing.

Wingshooters point and swing through their target, but generally the turkey shooter takes aim at the bird as if using a rifle. It's paramount that turkey hunters learn the point of impact of the pattern in relation to the point of aim. A dense shot pattern at distances up to 40 yards is important, but the pattern is all for naught if the shooter doesn't know where the center of the pattern strikes.

Equally important when taking aim is to practice in as many hunt-like situations as you can create. Some of these are:

1. Shooting while sitting down.
2. Shooting from awkward positions while sitting down.
3. Shooting with a facemask on.
4. Shooting in poor light conditions.
5. Judging distances with your mask on and in poor light, in timber and across open areas.
6. Learning point of aim in relation to point of impact.

7. Trying different loads, powder and shot at different distances with *your* turkey gun.

Build confidence and success as you take aim during the pre-season and learn where and how your gun shoots under all conditions.

Reading Sign

Successful turkey hunters rely on reading "sign." To determine whether or not turkeys are in an area, look for tracks, droppings, molted feathers, dusting areas, or scratchings, which provide clues to the bird's sex, age, and direction of travel. Fresh sign is assurance that turkeys are in the area.

Look for tracks in mud, snow, or sandy loam soils. A single track measuring in excess of 4½ inches from the tip of the middle toe to the heel pad is likely a tom; less than that, a hen.

Droppings of wild turkeys closely resemble those of domestic chickens. They are generally dark green to black in color, tipped in white and the thickness of a lead pencil or larger. Gobbler droppings are cylindrical, J-shaped or formed like a cheese curl. Hen droppings appear spiraled or in a pile, somewhat like a piece of popcorn.

Primary wing feathers that are rounded and barred to the end denote adults, while pointed, barless tips show juvenile birds. Buff- or white-tipped breast feathers indicate hens. Black-tipped, ensure toms.

Aging Your Turkey

Aging a gobbler in the field can be a challenge, but the more turkeys you see the better trained your eye will become. For a better idea as to how old an approaching longbeard may be, it's best to observe three features of the bird.

TURKEY TIPS
by Rob Keck

READING SIGN

A single track measuring more than $4\frac{1}{4}$ inches from the tip of the middle toe to the heel pad was likely made by a tom; less than that, a hen.

Droppings of wild turkeys closely resemble those of domestic chickens. They are generally dark green to black, tipped in white, and the thickness of a lead pencil or larger. Gobbler droppings are cylindrical, J-shaped or formed like a cheese curl. Hen droppings appear spiraled or in a pile –– somewhat like a piece of popcorn.

(Credit: Rob Keck)

First, the length of spurs on a gobbler is considered one of the most reliable characteristics in determining the age of a gobbler. Spurs will show some wear differences depending on the subspecies and habitat but generally they keep getting longer and sharper as the turkey ages.

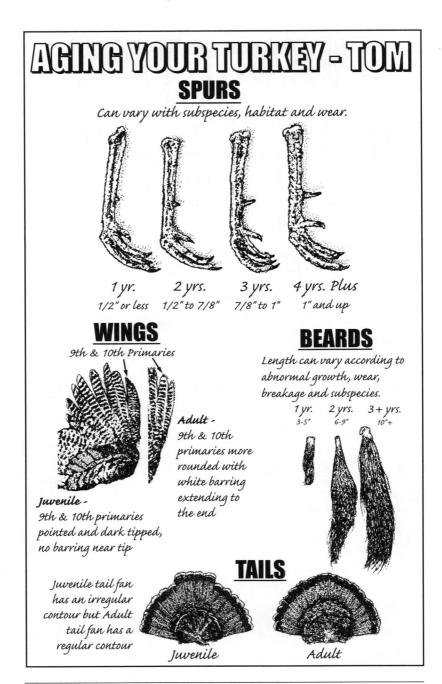

AGING YOUR TURKEY - TOM

SPURS

Can vary with subspecies, habitat and wear.

1 yr.	*2 yrs.*	*3 yrs.*	*4 yrs. Plus*
1/2" or less	*1/2" to 7/8"*	*7/8" to 1"*	*1" and up*

WINGS
9th & 10th Primaries

*Adult -
9th & 10th
primaries more
rounded with
white barring
extending to
the end*

*Juvenile -
9th & 10th primaries
pointed and dark tipped,
no barring near tip*

BEARDS

*Length can vary according to
abnormal growth, wear,
breakage and subspecies.*

1 yr.	*2 yrs.*	*3 + yrs.*
3-5"	*6-9"*	*10"+*

TAILS

*Juvenile tail fan
has an irregular
contour but Adult
tail fan has a
regular contour*

Juvenile   *Adult*

(Credit: Rob Keck)

Beard length is another variable used in determining the age of a gobbler. Beards generally grow at a rate of 4 inches to 5 inches a year and never stop growing. They normally get wider and thicker as the gobbler ages. Knowing this, you can be fairly certain that a gobbler with a less than 5-inch beard is about a one-year-old bird. Beard length is only helpful to a degree in determining the age of a gobbler, however. After a bird reaches the age of two, the beard reaches a length of 9 to 10 inches and it starts to wear down at the tip.

And finally, keep an eye on the gobbler's tail feathers. Tail feathers are useful in determining the age of a strutting gobbler since you can identify the bird as mature or not from a long distance. A jake's tailfeathers, the middle 2 to 5 sets of primary feathers are normally 2 to 4 inches longer than the rest. The juvenile tail fan has the irregular contour, unlike the adult tail fan with a regular contour.

When you're in the field, study these characteristics on every bird possible. Train your eye to notice spurs, tail feathers and beards.

Defensive Hunting

Keep in mind that it's never too early to start thinking of safety in the woods. Turkey hunting will continue to be one of the safest hunting sports if each of us keeps the following in mind:

1. Hunt defensively. Select a large tree trunk, stump or rock wider than your shoulders and taller than your head to place your back against while calling.
2. Never wear red, white, or blue clothing since it could be mistaken for the colors of a gobbler's head. This includes socks, T-shirts or anything else that could be seen by another hunter.

3. Choose a calling spot in open timber, not in thick brush. Good camouflage clothing makes eliminating movement more important than concealment.
4. Always keep your hands and head camouflaged when calling.
5. When using decoys, never carry them where visible to other hunters.
6. Never wave to get another hunter's attention. Sitting still, call out in a loud, clear voice or cough to let him know you are near. His presence has already compromised your setup.

A Natural Blind

The trunk of a tree is a favorite natural turkey blind, but be sure that the base is wider than your shoulders and taller than your head. A large tree trunk provides a good backrest, breaks up a hunter's outline and provides a commanding view when sitting upright. In this position, a hunter also can maneuver his gun when the turkey's head is behind another object. If the bird circles, a hunter can pivot around the tree's base to get a shot.

Small brush tops, netting and even ground blinds may be used in front of the hunter to provide additional concealment. Successful turkey hunters never disguise themselves in too much blind and are always in position for instant action.

Pick a Seat

Turkey hunters often times set up in mighty unusual and uncomfortable places. From wet bottomland bogs to rocky mountain ridges to snow-covered peaks, a turkey hunter must always be prepared to sit still and with patience.

Sitting in uncomfortable positions, however, makes for a terrible experience. For years I have relied on either a turkey vest with a seat cushion or a chair sold by the NWTF called the Lo-Boy Lite Turkey Hunting Chair. The vest and attached

BOOT BOTTOMS

Complete camo? You betcha! A quick check finds the turkey hunter with a _camo_ cap, coat, pants, face covering, gloves, socks, undergarments, gun and boots. The list seems complete, but have you checked your boot bottoms? Those new boots may be the dead giveaway to that tough old tom this spring, even if everything else is right.

Many boots come from the box with white, cream or light colored bottoms. Chances are, that while sitting, waiting for the bird to show up, your boot bottoms will be facing that approaching tom. The results can be disheartening.

Take those light colored soles and paint them or muddy'em so to break up that large expanse of unbroken white bottom. Considering a foot my size that expanse is about $4\frac{1}{2}$ " x 14", much larger than an ungloved hand or shiny face. Camo those boot bottoms, you'll be glad you did.

(Credit: Rob Keck)

cushion make for a light ground seat and the Lo-Boy chair is made of sturdy aluminum and a nylon-webbed seat, which is easy to carry over your shoulder. In addition, the seat adds several, sometimes critical inches of elevation. The angular design comfortably elevates the knee so that the gun can rest on top. Pick a seat that will help you become a better hunter and definitely make your wait on "Ole Tom" more enjoyable.

Knowing When to Move

Over the years I've had the thrill of watching good friends make wonderful shots on turkeys because they were ready and knew when to move.

If you're a right-handed shooter, practice pointing your left shoulder toward the turkey, having your knees up with the gun propped on the left one, with the gun butt pressed against your shoulder. More importantly, learn to watch the gobbler's head. Stay alert and attuned to the advance of an approaching gobbler by marking gobbles, drumming and footsteps. Only move when the tom's eyes are out of sight and anticipate the turkey's move. Inattentiveness or quick drawing will no doubt result in lost birds, so be ready and know when to move.

Key Off the Green

The first green of spring is a favorite color of most turkey hunters. Concentrations of turkeys are magnetized to spring's first signs of vegetation such as winter wheat and rye, clovers, and other green shoots. For a successful early season hunt, focus your hunting attention in areas associated near creeks or other wet areas. Certain acreages that have been burned in the off-season will also produce lush greenery along with specially planted and agricultural areas.

Many NWTF chapters, the U.S. Forest Service, corporate landowners, and sportsmen plant and improve open areas that directly benefit the wild turkey and its habitat. Concentrate on the first green of spring for a successful turkey hunt.

Standard Equipment

The standard equipment used by most turkey hunters includes camouflage clothing, gloves, head net, vest, boots, seat, shotgun and loads, and a variety of calls. One piece of gear that is often times forgotten, though, is a set of pruners, clippers, or shears.

Many times I'll find a spot to set up and call, only to find briars, vines, saplings, and major limbs in the way of a clear shooting lane. With a set of pruners, clearing vegetation is quick and easy.

I prefer the ratchet-cut type sold by the NWTF because it can take on much larger diameter limbs than most. The ratchet principle literally ratchets the blade through the limb. No matter what brand or style you choose, make sure a set of pruners becomes standard equipment in your turkey vest.

Match Your Peg

One of the most commonly misunderstood pieces of turkey calling equipment is the peg, which is used as a striker on slate and aluminum-type callers.

Not all pegs produce the same sound even though they might look the same. Differences in tone quality are due in part to the variations of densities, weights, tolerances, and materials that vary in pegs of a single brand or style.

Be sure to match the peg with the slate and vice versa to maximize the ultimate potential of the caller. Unfortunately, some commercially produced callers will not match and it's up to the individual to make the two more compatible by adjusting the peg.

Generally, pegs are made of two parts, the rod and the cap. Assuming the rod is not fixed, adjust the length of the exposed

TURKEY TIPS
by Rob Keck

MATCH YOUR PEG

The peg is an often misunderstood calling implement. Not all pegs produce the same sound, even though they might look the same. Variations of tone are largely due to variations of materials. Densities, weights, and tolerances may even vary in pegs of a single brand or style.

Generally pegs are made of two parts: The rod and the cap. Assuming the rod is not fixed, adjust the length of the exposed rod until you arrive at a length that produces the right sound with your slate.

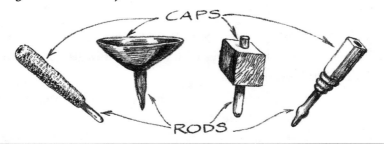

(Credit: Rob Keck)

rod until it produces the right sound. Matching your peg to the slate will give you the quality call you need for a successful turkey hunt.

Code of Ethics

Turkey hunters like to think of themselves as class members of the hunting fraternity. As new hunters enter the sport, and as the crossover from deer, waterfowl, and upland game hunting occurs, it's our responsibility as sensible turkey hunters to provide guidelines to the participants.

Long ago, the leaders of the NWTF took on the challenge of developing "A Wild Turkey Hunter's Code of Ethics." The following are words we as turkey hunters all can live by:

> As a wild turkey hunter and sportsman, I will hunt the wild turkey fairly; I will insist on a good shot; I will handle firearms safely; I will obey and support all game laws; I will respect the land and the landowner; I will avoid interfering with other hunters; I will appreciate the beauty of the wild turkey; I will share responsible wild turkey hunting with others; and I will work for wild turkey conservation.

Pinpointing Your Gobbler before Opening Day

By John Trout, Jr.

Full-time outdoor writer John Trout, Jr. has pursued the wild turkey throughout much of North America. His work has been published in almost every national publication and he is the author of seven books, including The Lyons Press book, The Complete Book of Wild Turkey Hunting, *which was published in 2000.*

I f you're wondering why it's so important to pattern a gobbler, I can tell you in just a few words. Many gobblers are called to each spring and don't come in because the hunter set up in the wrong location. On the other hand, if these hunters knew where the gobbler wanted to go to meet up with Ms. Right, they would probably triple their chance of bagging the turkey.

Let me give you an example of how I once failed to learn the habits of a gobbler.

When I began turkey hunting more than twenty-five years ago, it seemed that the only pre-season requirement was to hear a turkey. Today, many hunters still feel this way. If they hear a turkey, they assume the bird will provide them with a calling opportunity on opening morning. Perhaps that's why I felt so confident the first year that I hunted turkeys. After hearing a gobbler serenading in a nearby valley, I vowed to return and hunt him on opening morning.

A few days later I found myself standing in the precise location where I had heard the bird before the season opened. Sure enough, the bird gobbled just as the sun peeked over the eastern horizon. He was only about 200 yards from where I had heard him days earlier, and he sounded as eager as always. Without hesitation, I moved closer, set up and sent him a string of the sweetest hen yelps that I was capable of. He acknowledged my call with a double gobble, and I prematurely began patting myself on the back for a job well done.

Shortly after the bird left the roost, though, he began moving away from me. He was courteous enough to gobble a few times as he did, but, as most turkey hunters know, there is little satisfaction in gobbles that keep getting farther away.

Believe it or not, I attempted to kill the same turkey for couple of more days. He always eluded me, and he always seemed to end up in the same place—a nearby field. Sometimes it was an hour after dawn when he arrived at the field, and other times it was two hours after leaving the roost.

The moral to the preceding story is clear. I never patterned the gobbler, and I never came close to killing him. However, since my opening year failure, I have often made it a point to learn the habits of the gobbler that I would soon bump heads with. The reasons for doing so are obvious.

To determine where a gobbler is going, use a locator call to force him to talk. (Credit: John Trout, Jr.)

Like most turkey hunters, I want to call a turkey into range. Nonetheless, this is sometimes impossible to do if you don't know the habits of the gobbler you are pursuing. For instance, you can sound like the loveliest hen in the county, and you can call at the right times, but this doesn't matter if a gobbler wants to go the other way. And, believe me, a large percentage of the gobblers that are called to each spring do just that.

First, consider that the gobblers fully expect the hens to come to them. Some don't have the patience to wait, and for that, many of us are grateful. In fact, many of the birds that don't wait on the hens are two-year-olds. However, if the hunter can make it a point to be where the turkey wants to go, which is usually where the gobbler will have the best chance of picking up a girlfriend, he will increase his odds of bringing home a bird, and particularly a dominant one.

Roost Sites

Patterning a gobbler should begin where he roosts. It may or may not end there, however. Some birds are easier to bag than others are after leaving the roost simply because they are more dependable. Nonetheless, it is vitally important to learn the habits of a gobbler before the hunting season begins, and a hunter must find out just *how dependable* the gobbler is.

I won't say too much about finding roost sites. You probably already know that nothing beats hearing gobbles when you must positively identify a roost site. Feathers and droppings also provide indications of a roosting site, but hearing the turkey just days before the hunting begins will provide you with tell-tale proof that he's there.

However, I will discuss the importance of being in the right location when you spend your pre-season morning listening for gobbles. Always select the best vantage point from which to listen for him. In some locations, you will hear the turkey when he is in the tree gobbling, but this does little to pattern the bird. Very few birds fly down and land within gun range of the caller. Most are killed after the gobbler has been down for a while and has moved a given distance. For this reason, if you can't hear him once he's on the ground and moving, there is no way to learn the habits of the turkey you will soon try to call up.

For starters, I select a high point or an open field. That is, taking into consideration that the wind isn't howling. Hilltop and open areas are not good points to listen from when the wind blows. If breezy conditions exist, I will get into the timber or move below the top of a ridge to listen for gobbles.

Once a bird begins gobbling, you might find it necessary to move closer, but do so cautiously. Your chances of hearing the bird after he's on the ground will depend on how close you are, and you want to be as close as possible.

After the turkey flies down, expect a quiet period. He may not gobble for several minutes. After hitting the ground, most birds want to snatch up a little grit and sometimes feed for a while. This is a normal activity and not a sign that they don't want to gobble. Many gobblers will remain silent for only a brief period. The availability of hens might also affect the gobbling. If they come running to him, he may or may not continue gobbling.

You can count on a gobbler moving somewhere shortly after landing. To pattern the turkey effectively, you must know his directional travel. Since this is only possible if he gobbles, use a locator call every few minutes, but avoid being too persistent. However, avoid using hen calls to make a turkey talk. Hen calls should never be used before opening day. For this reason, I suggest you carry more than one type of locator call. For instance, if owl hooters don't get the job done, consider a crow call or another type of locating device.

Once you know the turkey's travel route, make it a point to come back another morning. Many gobblers may not travel a distinct route, but they usually travel in a general direction. If the turkey you have listened to travels to the northeast, you should make it a point to be on the northeast side of his roost area before you begin calling on opening morning. Surprisingly, if you are on the wrong side of his travel route, he may hang up and gobble, hoping to convince you to come to him.

After pinpointing a gobbler's travel route, make it a point to learn the terrain he travels. I once patterned a bird that walked the same ridge each morning. When opening day arrived, I set up too far below the bird. The turkey attempted to get to me but was reluctant to cross a fence that I didn't know was there. He could have easily walked under or flown over the fence, but gobblers are finicky when they approach hen talk. For this reason, always walk the area thoroughly to locate fences, creeks, ravines, and thickets that may stop a bird from getting to you. These obstacles can cost you even if you set up in front of a gobbler that wants to move toward you.

Strutting Zones

Gobblers frequently visit strutting zones within an hour or two of leaving the roost. If the hunters know where the strutting zone is, they will increase their chances of harvesting the bird later in the morning after the gobbling begins to subside.

Before going on, let me say that not all gobblers will visit strutting zones daily. Naturally, a tom turkey will not walk away from breeding hens just to go somewhere and strut unless he's a young gobbler and is afraid of a dominant bird. More than likely, he will follow the hens to wherever they want to go. I'll discuss these locations in just a moment.

Just how difficult is it to locate a strutting zone? Sometimes it's easy, and other times it's difficult. Many hunters will find such areas before the hunting begins. During the season, hunters might be led to a strutting zone by a gobbler they attempt to call in. I have had this happen on numerous occasions, and I always make it a point to take advantage of the strutting zone on another day.

Before the hunting season, when you're busy patterning a gobbler that's just left the roost, all you need to do is keep moving with the turkey. This is easy to do if the turkey frequently gobbles. If you determine he is still moving, you can assume that he has not yet arrived at a strutting zone.

If the bird stays in one location for twenty or thirty minutes, you can assume he has probably arrived at the strutting zone. Just how much he gobbles once he's there will vary. Some turkeys will continue gobbling after they arrive, but I've found that most will gobble less than they did as they traveled to the strutting zone.

You can find strutting zones in various areas. The edges of fields, small openings in the middle of timber, tops of ridges and old roadbeds are typical strutting zones. Upon inspecting a strutting zone, you will usually find marks in the dirt, or you will find disturbed leaves caused by the birds' wings as they drag the ground. If terrain permits, you might also find numerous tracks and droppings.

Just how long a bird will stay in a strutting zone is dependent upon several factors. Consider that he hopes to attract hens. If he does, he may follow them away. If not, he may spend several hours here, moving away into cooler areas only when the temperature rises. For this reason, if you do locate a strutting zone and your early-morning strategy fails, don't be afraid to spend your midmorning hours near the strutting zone.

Nesting Sites

Not a spring hunting season goes by where I don't hear hunters complain about hens accompanying gobblers. That's understandable, particularly since I have done my share of moaning over the years. Even when many of the breeding hens are incubating, there are usually plenty of non-breeding jennies in the woods to accompany the gobblers. However, if the hunter is aware of those areas where hens will nest, they will usually find gobblers hanging around.

Typically, hens will go to their nests daily before incubating begins, usually during midmorning hours. If a gobbler joins with the hen in the early morning, and he often does, you can bet your luckiest hunting hat he will follow her to the nest. It is for this reason that hunters should have some idea of where the hens will go.

Hens will nest in a variety of areas, but usually they are located where there is plenty of cover. Cutover areas are favorites because of numerous logjams. Overgrown powerline areas are also preferred, as are brushy fields and brushpiles.

Although I prefer to pattern gobblers by knowing the location of strutting zones and their directional travel upon leaving the roost, nesting sites are excellent places to be late in the morning. Even when the breeding hens leave the gobblers to lay eggs, the gobblers will often stay there hoping to join up with juvenile hens.

Feeding and Dusting Areas

Finding feeding and dusting areas is probably the least productive patterning tactic. However, I didn't say these areas were not productive; on the contrary, these areas are often the place to be—if and when you encounter tight-mouthed gobblers. And let's face it, at some point during the season—particularly in the late season—you probably will.

After the hunting pressure increases, turkeys often stop gobbling shortly after leaving the roost or immediately after hitting the ground. Nevertheless, when turkeys don't talk, you can bet they are still in the same areas where you heard them previously. They will feed and dust daily close to where they were early in the season. Even if the gobblers are with hens, the hens will lead them to these areas. For this reason, the hunter should locate both feeding areas and dusting areas. I practice this patterning method both before and during the hunting season.

Heavily scratched areas are solid indications of feeding areas, but make certain when you inspect them that the scratchings are fresh. It's not always difficult to find scratchings in the hardwoods, but only those that were recently made will do you any good. You might also want to observe fields, since turkeys often visit open areas to feed on insects and seeds.

Dusting bowls are obvious. The dusting sites are large, sometimes 3 feet or more in diameter, and they often contain feathers and tracks. Look for them along the fringes of fields, on old roadbeds, around ponds and anywhere else where they can get to dry soil.

Once you've located feeding areas and dusting sites, you should get to them shortly after the birds leave the roost. Once there, make certain you can remain comfortable. I've often spent a couple of hours at these locations. Feeding areas and dusting sites have rewarded me on a few occasions during the late season.

Touchy Business

Patterning a gobbler is touchy business. You must make certain you don't spoil a hunt before it begins. Moreover, there are two ways you can spoil your hunt. First, turkeys might detect your presence one too many times. This could cause them to change their habits. Secondly, you could spoil your hunt by thinking you have patterned a gobbler when you haven't.

To avoid being detected, you should use common sense and not get too close for comfort. That goes for roost sites in particular. I can remember on one occasion having to hide behind a logjam as three gobblers walked by minutes after they left the roost tree. That was too close. Make it a point to stay within hearing distance but not close enough to be spotted. In addition, if the woods haven't greened up, you must be extra cautious. This is particularly true if you try to follow a moving gobbler.

Always be certain you have indeed patterned a gobbler. Usually, one pre-season trip to the woods won't get the job done. If you want to learn the habits of a gobbler, I would suggest you make two or three attempts. Finally, never assume that a gobbler is totally dependable. He may do something on one day, only to do something else on another. That's why I'm never happy pinpointing just one gobbler. When it comes to patterning gobblers before opening day, one is good, two is better, and three is best.

Afternoon Delight

The Pluses of Hunting Turkeys in the P.M.

By Jim Casada

Jim Casada is a full-time freelancer who has written or edited more than thirty books and upwards of three thousand magazine articles for Sporting Classics *and* Turkey & Turkey Hunting. *A past president of the Outdoor Writers Association of America, he has won more than one hundred regional or national awards for his writing and photography.*

It happened well over a decade ago, but in looking back on a lot of marvelously misspent hours devoted to the quest for His Majesty, the wild gobbler, two moments in that season in the mid-1980s were defining points in my ongoing evolution as a turkey hunter. The first came in my home state of South Carolina, where good fortune and reasonable annual dues had given me access to 1500 acres of prime turkey terrain in a club where most members were exclusively interested in whitetails. The second, a fortnight later, was an enjoyable outing with Harold Knight in his "home stomping grounds" of Land Between the Lakes along the Kentucky-Tennessee border.

I already considered myself a moderately accomplished turkey hunter, with twenty-odd toms and a world of frustration and futility on my ledger. Up to that point, however, every bird I had killed had been taken in the morning, with all but a couple of them making their last gobble in the first two hours of the day. Sporadically I had gone afield in the afternoon, more with peace and solitude, maybe a sun-drenched nap, and roosting a bird uppermost in my mind. I really didn't consider afternoon hunting much of a viable option. That afternoon on the hunt club acres planted serious seeds of doubt about such notions.

At my first set up spot, a gobbler showed up within minutes of my first call. He never gobbled, but the rustling of dry leaves, followed by the unmistakably alluring sound of drumming, alerted me to the bird's presence. Scarcely an hour after that initial encounter, a second tom came at a full run in response to a few plaintive notes from my trusty wingbone. He never slowed down until he was within 30 yards, and on top of that, he ran counter to standard wisdom in that his path to me brought him straight down a steep hill.

Everyone should be blessed with the occasional day of that sort, although the other thing which made the afternoon so memorable was anything but a blessing. I missed both turkeys, and such times of tragedy have a way of locking themselves away in memory's vaults. Maybe it was the shock of seeing gobblers in range in the afternoon, but more likely it was just two closely spaced examples of this scribe's outstanding ability to miss turkeys.

The second experience came with Harold Knight, and not once but several times, while "cutting and running" along the ridge lines of Land Between the Lakes, he managed to get turkeys to gobble. We finished the hunt empty-handed, but I left it convinced that by overlooking afternoon hunting I had, for years, denied myself one of turkey hunting's great delights. It is also arguably, in the wider scheme of turkey hunting, the sport's most underutilized opportunity. With such thoughts in mind, what follows is a detailed look at the P.M. pursuit of gobblers, seen mainly through the experienced eyes of Harold Knight.

Techniques for Afternoon Hunting

"There are several approaches to hunting gobblers in the afternoon which I have found effective over the years," Harold

Harold Knight at the end of a successful afternoon hunt.
(Credit: Jim Casada)

Knight says. His favorite tactic, one which he has honed to a razor-sharp edge over many years, is to do what he describes, quite simply, as "covering ground." This can be done in a variety of fashions, but the basic intent in every case is to call within earshot of a lot of gobblers. You are looking for that tom, and it may only be one out of twenty birds, which is alone and anxious for female company.

The lazy way to accomplish this is to drive back country roads, particularly in ridge-and-valley country, stopping at every likely spot to call. This is "cutting and running" at its fastest, and there is no better way to cover ground. There are negatives, however, among them being the quite real possibility of disturbing turkeys which might otherwise have been receptive or the chance that you will be caught with your "pants down," so to speak, when a turkey answers close by.

Knight prefers to do this type of hunting by walking. "I'll hunt ridges," he says, "cutting and calling loudly every time I come to a spot which appeals to me. It might be a good listening post, a likely strutting ground, a place I've dealt with birds before, or maybe just a location which strikes my fancy." Knight normally cutts and calls quite loudly in such situations. "My hope is to get a tom to answer, sometimes in spite of himself. If I can locate a bird, then I can plan my strategy from that point."

While walking ridges, Knight relies on his ears at least as much as he does on calling. "You've got to listen carefully," he remarks. "Often you can be fooled by distorted gobbler sounds. There is more external noise, particularly of a manmade sort, in the afternoon. You will hear traffic, winds tend to get up more as you move later in the day, and it is a time of year when all nature's creatures are especially noisy."

Knight also points to the fact that the savvy hunter will be closely attuned to sounds other than gobbling. "Turkeys just don't gobble as much in the afternoon," he comments, "al-

says. "He is usually with hens, but there are a lot of things you can try to bring him within range. The key is really the hens, because he is going to go wherever they do." To get them coming his way, Knight often turns to some soft yelps and purrs, just loud enough to pique a hen's curiosity. "If she comes to investigate, you can bet the old boy will tag right along behind her. I love to see a big tom waddle along as he tries to keep up and strut at the same time."

Speaking of loving to watch birds, that is another reason Knight especially enjoys going after field gobblers in the afternoon. "You always learn something when you get to watch turkeys," he reasons, "and when the whole show is in front of you it is also possible to make key decisions such as relocating or 'cutting 'em off at the pass.'" With field gobblers it is often possible to deal with a bird for an entire afternoon without ever hearing a gobble, but at least as the drama unfolds the hunter sees it happen.

Some Thoughts on Calls and Calling

Like any old-time hunter, Knight has developed some strong opinions on what types of calling are most effective for afternoon birds. "If I am trying to provoke a gobble," he says, "I not only like to call loud; I like to use a call with a high pitch. The boat paddle-type call is a good choice, as are aluminum-type slates such as our Ultimate Series call. Whatever type calling you try though, don't get into a routine. By sticking to any one routine you are hurting yourself. When you change, sooner or later you will hit on what he wants. And as I've said before, he's serious if he gobbles, especially more than once, in the afternoon."

When Knight discourses on afternoon hunting as a whole, and his sentiments are those echoed by others who have discovered its undoubted rewards, his thoughts are reminiscent of a smash country hit of a couple of decades back entitled "Afternoon Delight." While the lyrics of the song referred to delights of a type quite different from those afforded by the rites of spring, it could have been a turkey hunter's theme song. It began with "Started out this morning getting so excited" and evolved to the theme of afternoon delight. Any hunter who hasn't sampled the pleasures to be found in the P.M. is missing something, and as Harold Knight says, "there is something really special about the challenge of afternoon toms, and if you take a nice tom at that time of day there is plenty of reason to be proud."

Turkey Talkin' Secrets

By Kathy Etling

Kathy Etling has hunted from her native Missouri to the high country and deserts of the West. She has been a regular contributor to Outdoor Life, American Hunter, *and has authored numerous books with The Lyons Press, including* Hunting Superbucks, Cougar Attacks, *and* The Quotable Cowboy.

I f you're a bona fide turkey hunter, then you are well-acquainted with the feeling of frustration. If you're a bona fide turkey hunter, you just know, sometimes, that you'll be going home birdless yet again. This is the feeling I had in my gut after enduring almost two days of futile turkey hunting. The birds were gobbling, all right. They just weren't coming in to any calls, at least any calls that one of the country's premier turkey callers was producing. And, believe me, I'm not referring to myself.

I was hunting near my Osage Beach, Missouri home with the renowned Ralph Duren, turkey caller *extraordinaire*. Heck, Ralph isn't just a turkey caller; if it's an animal, bird or reptile—

and it makes a sound—Ralph can mimic it. Ralph's calls usually sound better than those made by the real McCoys, too. He's nothing short of phenomenal in his ability to replicate every sound in nature. The only thing that wasn't phenomenal, during our almost two days together, was the number of longbeards that had scampered to within shotgun range. So far, that was a big zero.

I'd become used to being startled by an assortment of animal calls erupting nearby. The pileated woodpecker was the first, and almost the last. Ralph let fly with that one while he was a mere 2 feet from my ear. Ralph hadn't meant to scare me out of my one wit; he was merely trying to locate a gobbler.

As the hours passed, Ralph resorted to much of the firepower in his game-calling arsenal: the call of a bobwhite, a keening red-tailed hawk, various and sundry owls, a coyote, a cote of lovestruck doves. Whenever he saw a squirrel, he'd talk to the animal; Ralph didn't seem to be able to help himself. Why should he? This man is able to create, with his mouth alone, the calls of sixty different animals and birds. Even more amazing, in my limited experience spent hunting with Ralph, was that the animals usually talked back—and paid us a visit! Except the one we were after: the incredibly uncooperative mature tom turkey.

A woodpecker flashed through the woods. A hawk keened and circled above our heads. Squirrel bedlam began in earnest as branches swayed above our heads. But Mr. Tom, well, he wasn't fooled. "Sometimes, you can't buy a good gobble," Ralph said, in disgust, after a trio of jakes sauntered by within 15 feet of us. I knew exactly what he meant.

Ralph Duren works for the Missouri Department of Conservation. Ralph is not just an employee; he's a goodwill specialist. He visits classrooms, garden and hunting clubs, conducts shows and seminars, and has even been a guest on "The Tonight Show" with Jay Leno. David Letterman had Ralph scheduled, but canceled him at the last minute. Dave made a major mistake, because if there's one thing Ralph Duren can do, besides make the most realistic game calls I've ever heard, it's entertain people.

At this point in our hunt, though, Ralph had given up trying to entertain me. He was doing his best to get the unwilling participant in the day's contest to gobble. It didn't seem as though that was likely to happen, even though he'd tried every locator call he knew. In fact, we'd just about given up for the day. The field we were striding through was green and lush with new growth brome and orchardgrass. A crow cawed and carried on, but I knew it was Ralph. A hawk screamed, but ditto. Ralph then threw back his head and howled like a lovesick coyote. Somewhere, far off in the distance, a turkey gobbled.

"Longbeard," Ralph said. He then began cutting and yelping, churning up the brisk April air with a variety of hen turkey sounds guaranteed to fill a gobbler's breast with lust. The tom wasn't buying any of it. Not a peep he made. "Well, let's give him what he wants," Ralph said, just before yapping sharply four or five times, then howling a long, mournful masterpiece of a howl—all with his natural voice! What else from the man who's won numerous voice competitions such as the National Wild Turkey Federation's Grand National Gobbling championship?

The turkey again answered the coyote call, even though the time was pushing 11 A.M. "Let's get ready," Ralph said. "That old boy is coming!" We rushed to the field's edge where Ralph set up against a tree about 12 feet behind me. He cutt softly, cackled a bit, then let fly with a few muffled yelps. The tom gobbled! The bird was now less than 100 yards away and closing fast. As I thought that to myself, the tom came running up the hill, made a sharp right, then half-ran, half-strutted to the spot out in the velvety grass where Ralph had hastily staked out a decoy.

Trees obscured my view of the bird until the last second when the gobbler was almost too close to hit. I'm sure Ralph

*The author and Ralph Duren admire her fine
longbeard.* (Credit: Kathy Etling)

was praying to the turkey gods that this crazy woman fire, and
quickly. As the tom cleared the final obstacle to a clear shot, I
shot. The longbeard expired in a sorry wad of deflated feathers.

Ralph Duren is one of the most productive turkey callers
and hunters in the country. This is why he is in great demand
from March until May, wherever open seasons may beckon
him. While we may have had our problems on this occasion,

despite the use of at least a dozen different locator calls, the man has tricks up his sleeve that even he occasionally forgets.

Like the gobbler fight. "If there are gobblers nearby and they're answering, but won't budge toward you, try staging a gobbler fight," Ralph said. "If they're with hens, the prevailing belief is that there isn't much you can do. But there's nothing a wily old tom enjoys more than being a spectator at a good gobbler fight. I use a wing flapper, my slate call and my voice, although others use a mouth call, to make every kind of purr, gobble, half-gobble, and aggressive cutt I can produce. A lot of wing-flapping is critical to a staged fight. When toms are aggravated, they really go to town beating at each other with their wings. Last spring, when the birds were being particularly balky, I used this tactic and a big old gobbler came charging right in. My hunter couldn't believe it. 'I wouldn't have known what to do,' he said. 'It sounded to me like those birds were leaving and nothing was going to change their minds.' "

Ralph also believes in staying out until the day's hunting ends. "I like to wait for those 10 o'clock birds," he said. "Most folks go home at 8:30 A.M., or as soon as the birds get close-mouthed."

When it comes to talkin' turkey, there's no better talkers than the two men who tell us their turkey talkin' secrets here. Beginning with Ralph Duren of Jefferson City, Missouri, and then proceeding to Butch McElwain of Cadiz, Kentucky, each relies on his own special brand of turkey-talkin' secrets.

Butch, owner and operator of Whitetail Creek Outfitters, would rather be guiding turkey and deer hunters than hunting himself, and, I suspect, even more than breathing. When it comes to calling, few are better. He's won major elk and goose and turkey calling national championships, too, although you'd have to hogtie the man to drag this information from him. Yet as fine a caller as Butch is, what he looks for when he's out scouting turkeys is a place that lends itself to little or no calling.

"I look for really remote places," Butch said. "No roads nearby, no homes, really off-the-beaten-path locales. The ideal spot will have a nice pine thicket where turkeys seem to prefer to roost. Maybe some bottom ground where birds can fly down to right off the roost. Remote locales are where you'll most likely find older, wiser birds—what I call 'bonus' birds. A turkey that's survived several hunting seasons isn't going to spend his time gobbling his head off. He's going to be very cagey about when he does his gobbling, *if* he gobbles at all. But these three-, four-, five-year and older birds are what I'm after, so I adapt my hunting methods to suit them."

To that end, Butch heads into the backcountry. "Those older birds don't want to hang around where there's lots of hunting pressure," he explained. "At least that's what I've discovered. And if I'm hunting these educated turkeys, birds that have heard everything at least once, I'll get in there early when I'm scouting, then sit down and listen. I'll let the gobblers tell me where they go, and what turns them on. Older, wiser turkeys will often just fly out of the roost and keep on going. What I'm listening for is the direction in which they fly. Then I'll hike toward that spot and search quietly for old logging roads the birds may be following, open places where they may be strutting, or ridges that they may be feeding along later in the morning. Discovering travel routes and patterns is more than half the battle. You can often do this quite effectively by merely looking over the terrain and its features."

Talking turkey, in this instance, means "talking" the barest of minimums. Once Butch gets settled down in a place where he believes that old tom is likely to be headed, he won't call a lot because to do so signals to the wise old bird a human hunter could very well be in his neck of the woods. No, he'll call very little and softly, just enough to let the old boy know he's there and he's willing, though a smidgen shy. "Get their interest, be where they're wanting to go, and get ready," Butch advises.

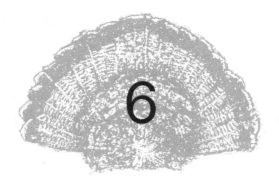

Quick Tip: Take to the Trees for Gobblers

By Peter J. Fiduccia

Peter J. Fiduccia is editor-in-chief of the Outdoorsman's Edge Book Club, consulting editor of Whitetail Hunting Strategies *magazine, and host of the nationally acclaimed* Woods 'n' Waters *television show. He lives in Warwick, New York.*

Not only could I hear the tom gobbling as he picked his way through the underbrush, I could also see him as he approached. Every now and then he would stop and pace back and forth before continuing toward me. The dense cover gave him the confidence to keep coming. He was 75 yards from me; he would soon see my hen decoy.

The gobbler entered the underbrush that skirted the woodlot and, spotting the hen, fanned his tail, gobbled, and started to strut. Undiscouraged by the hen's non-response, he circled her and brushed up against her. Confused, the bird stopped and just stood there, looking at the hen; as he did, I placed the crosshairs on the kill zone and fired.

Many hunters might not have been able to see the approach of the big tom as I did. In fact, they might not have seen the bird at all. I did, because I was watching all of the action from a tree stand.

A Revelation

Several years ago it occurred to me that I saw more turkeys from my tree stand during deer season than in spring. In developing a strategy the following spring, I discovered that by placing a tree stand in the thickest cover I could find, gobblers answered my calls and came into shooting range more frequently than when I was hunting on the ground. Mature birds, especially call-shy ones, obviously felt more comfortable responding and coming to hens through dense undergrowth.

Placement

Position your tree stand where there is background cover to break up your outline. A good backdrop can be a cluster of evergreens or a much larger oak tree. Having some type of camo cover skirted around the front and sides of your stand is also a good idea. This way, any last-minute movement of your leg, foot or lower arm is concealed.

Decoy Ploys

To divert a gobbler's attention from your position and lure him into gun range, place a decoy 30 yards from your stand. Decoys that move in the breeze are the most lifelike and work best for me. Placing two or three other decoys 10 to 15 yards from the main decoy helps complete the illusion. The extra decoys should be in the feeding position, whereas the main decoy should be in the alert and upright position.

Gobblers at High Noon

By Monte Burch

Monte Burch has been an outdoor writer for four decades and has authored more than fifty books and thousands of magazine articles. Some of his Lyons Press books include Field Dressing and Butchering Upland Birds, Waterfowl, and Wild Turkeys, The Ultimate Guide to Making Outdoor Gear and Accessories, *and* The Ultimate Guide to Calling and Decoying Waterfowl. *He lives in Missouri.*

The day gave little promise when Joe Drake and I left the opulent quarters of Cedar Heights Plantation in central Alabama. A fine drizzle filled the early morning darkness making it hard to leave the comfort of Joe's truck—only the promise of a big gobbler Joe had located the day before made me move. We slogged the red clay of a muddy logging road for a half mile as the weak early morning light slowly gathered. Once we reached the top of a low pine ridge, we stopped and Joe gave a guttural owl call. Nothing! The misty hills were as silent as a tomb. We continued our hike, frequently stopping to owl, then finally resorting to giving yelps, but still without success.

Then the rain came in earnest. We were a good 2 miles from the truck, so we headed for a nearby deer hunting "blind" on the plantation. Within minutes we were sitting comfortably in a snug wooden house, complete with sliding glass windows, propane heater and comfortable chairs while a toad strangler of a rainstorm blew outside. Typically, I was wetter inside my rain suit than out, but as we sat through the storm, the heater gradually began to dry us out. The problem was the storm simply didn't want to quit. Two hours, then three went by before the rain began to slack off. We decided to head back to the truck, repeating our "walk-and-call" routine. Unfortunately, part way to the truck the rain began again and we reached the truck drowned and frustrated and ready to head back for dry clothes and lunch. Half way back to the plantation headquarters the sun popped out and almost at the same time a huge gobbler ran across the road in front of us and into the plantation property.

Joe wisely continued on down the road a half mile before pulling over. We hit the ground running and after a mile circle were panting and puffing, but hopefully ahead of the big bird. Joe set up slightly behind me and when we were both ready he gave a series of yelps. A single muffled gobble answered and that was it. An hour later, without making a single sound, the gobbler strutted in. I took careful aim just below his softball white head and pulled the trigger of the Remington 1100 Mag. As Joe and I admired the trophy I glanced at my watch, "12:00 P.M., just in time for lunch," I noted.

12:00 P.M. gobblers can often be the easiest to take, although the same bird may have given you fits earlier in the day. Joe Drake, from Alabama, is one of the top contest callers in the country, a veteran turkey guide, and on the Advantage Pro Staff

Team. I've had the good fortune to hunt with him several times and each hunt has been a real learning experience.

"Lots of folks have to go to work after the first hour of daylight," Joe says. "But I always take my vacation during turkey season so I have all day to hunt. Turkeys are usually not as active or vocal during midday as they are during daylight or roosting time periods, unless you can get a bird fired up. Then they'll gobble as well during the middle of the day as any other time. At that time of the day I like to 'cutt' to a turkey to get them fired up. I walk along logging roads, or even drive from place to place, depending on what type of area I'm in. If I can use a vehicle, I will because you can cover so much more area. Stop, get out, and cutt. The first thing I do is crow call, I usually don't owl hoot during the middle of the day. If I don't get a response from the crow call, I'll cutt. Just before I get ready to go, I'll cutt two or three times. If I don't get an answer, I'll drive down the road another 200 or 300 yards to another likely spot, the top of a ridge, head of a big bottom, or something like that. Anything that I can get distance from. The main problem you have in the spring is you can get a lot of wind in the middle of the day, and you have to be close to hear a bird. A lot of times if you can't get birds to gobble, check out the pastures or clearcuts or down an old logging road. Turkeys like to be seen and they're going to be out in these clear areas strutting during midday. Usually in the wooded parts of the county you can just go along the logging roads and cutt.

"Gobblers will frequently be with the hens during the early morning hours. Perhaps they only have a couple of hens and they service them. By midmorning they're going to be looking for new hens and they'll come even more readily than during the early morning hours. I've left birds in the early morning, and gone back at 10 or 11:00 A.M.. It's often just like you're working a different bird.

This gobbler was taken midday, while strutting in a grassy clearing.
(Credit: Monte Burch)

"Quite often you'll work such a bird two or three hours. You yelp and he'll gobble, and you just finally give up on him. But go back during midday and hit him and the first thing you know, he's coming to you like a freight train."

Brad Harris, Public Relations Director of Outland Sports, a world class turkey hunter and a long time hunting buddy also offers some mighty good advice on 12:00 P.M. gobblers.

"I try to cover a lot of ground and call from the high points during midday," Brad says. "I like to call down hollers and down to benches where gobblers might be hanging out. I usually use really aggressive yelping and a lot of cutting for late morning birds. This is to get them to gobble back and give away their location. I'll make a series of cutts then follow it up with some real fast yelping, eight or ten notes. What you're trying to do is fire up a gobbler and get him to gobble, and quite often he will. Lots of times they may be a quarter of a mile or further away. I like to get them hot enough to gobble two or three times so I can pinpoint their location, then I'll know how to approach. Sometimes I'll even call to him as I'm going. That, however, can be a little tricky because he may try to meet you. You have to be extra careful because he may start coming to you even after your first call. At times I'll keep up the aggressive calling, other times I'll get in close and just call softly."

Brad and I had one such hunt in Kansas where we doubled on a couple of real trophies just after 12.00 P.M. "The real key is covering lots of ground and hitting the high points," Brad explained. "This is especially true hitting the places where you heard gobblers that morning. Hit those places again before you go home. Many times the hens will be gone or on their nest, the gobbler will be in the same general area, and you can fire him up.

"Another tactic if you're hunting with a partner is one person stay in the same spot you first heard the call and continue calling to keep the bird gobbling while the other hunter moves in on him. This allows the hunter to move in without making a call that might spook the bird while the hunter at the locator spot keeps the bird gobbling. The hunter slips in, sets up fast, and then gives just a few soft hen calls. Double teaming is a good tactic for late morning gobblers."

"Run and gun" tactics used for midday gobblers can have some disadvantages as well as dangers. Slipping along a ridge giving a few calls every few minutes or so can definitely help locate gobblers, but it can also unfortunately attract other hunters. It can also call in silent gobblers you never hear but slip in and often slip away after spotting you, or turn and run just out of gun range. Jakes or young gobblers will do this quite often. Two such incidents illustrate the problem. Several years ago Bill Harper and I were walking up an old logging road, headed back to our truck in the last few minutes of legal hunting time. We were hunting in Missouri, where hunting must stop at 1:00 P.M. Disgusted with a day of hearing almost no birds, we were walking along comparing calls. First he would call, then I'd give my version. Within 100 yards of my Chevy Suburban, I unshouldered my gun preparatory to unloading it and just happened to look in time to see a jake round a bend in the road, sprint past the truck and head our way like a race horse, kicking gravel and sand behind as he ran. It was comical to see him put his feet out in front in a full skid, almost like the Road Runner cartoon character, and at the last moment make a fast 90-degree turn into the brush at the side of the road.

Another time I was walking along the edge of a ridge with a steep rocky lip in Arkansas. It had been a tough morning and I tiredly leaned my gun against a handy tree, took out my mouth call, and gave a series of cutts and yelps hoping to locate a gobbler down on the mountain bench below me. I called and listened intently—nothing happened. Another series of calls, still silence. Then suddenly a huge white head popped over the rocks less than 10 feet in front of me. I don't know who was more surprised, me or the gobbler, but his reaction was definitely the fastest, and I watched a huge bearded bird disappear just as quickly as he appeared before I could even get my gun. It was a hard won lesson I won't forget soon.

The best tactic is to move from area to area, wearing a hunter orange garment as you move. Then set up in a good hunting spot before you make any calls. Remove the hunter orange, put on your face mask and gloves and get ready just as if you were working a turkey you had already located.

Aggressive calls such as cutting may be used to locate noontime gobblers. (Credit: Monte Burch)

One gobbler I will never forget came into my calls just a half hour before legal quitting time in Missouri. I was trying to get a gobbler for my good friend Joan Smith, and we had worked several gobblers all morning but with no luck. We heard a faint gobble in an area I hadn't hunted because I hadn't seen any sign. Just as we began to set up, a hen began to scold us, and she and I got into a pretty fierce argument. A huge, double-bearded gobbler walked silently in and Joan dropped him like a sack of salt.

Some states allow all day hunting and the midafternoon can also be a good time to locate lonely gobblers. Make sure, however, that you check the legal hunting times for the state you're hunting. Some states close at noon, some 1:00, and others allow hunting from morning to evening.

Some gobblers come hard, some easy. A big 24-pound gobbler I took at 12:30 was one of the easiest I've hunted, but it didn't start out that way in the morning. He gobbled strong on the roost and I set up and started a calling contest that lasted for almost two hours. In addition to the old gobbler, I could also hear hens along with him and finally gave up and headed to hunt another bird. Typically, the rest of the morning was dead silent as I covered several miles of ridges and hollers. Headed back home and following a ridge paralleling the one the vocal gobbler had been on, I gave a series of yelps and he again immediately answered with a double gobble. I ran down the mountainside hoping to get on the same ridge with him. Half way down I heard him gobble closer down on his mountainside, then a double gobble even closer. I desperately looked for a good spot to set up, got ready, gave one call, and he gobbled behind me going up the mountain I just left. We had passed each other on a dead run. I gave a couple of soft yelps and he gobbled again and came in almost in a dead run. Granted, 12:00 gobblers are not always that easy, but don't give up in the middle of the morning; you may be missing some of the best hunting of the day!

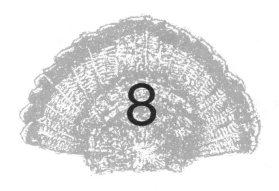

Out-of-Position Gobblers

Q & As on When and When Not to Move on a Gobbler

By John Phillips

John E. Phillips is an award-winning freelance writer, magazine editor, photographer, lecturer, outdoor consultant, marketing consultant and book author. Currently he is editor of Alabama Whitetail and Bass Magazine, *a field editor for* Game and Fish Publications and Vulcan Publications, *the Alabama and Florida editor for* Saltwater Sportsman Magazine, *and the editor-at-large for Harris Publications' outdoor magazines.*

Often, when a turkey comes in, you have to move to get off a shot. Although you've set up right, the turkey comes in wrong. Chris Kirby, president of Quaker Boy Calls, and I learned that lesson the hard way while hunting right outside of Orchard Park, New York. Instead of coming along the edge of the field like Kirby predicted, the gobbler came in to the middle of the thicket. To help me get off a shot, Kirby had to turn the gobbler around and march him within 10 feet of me. He accomplished that task by using Quaker Boy's new Gobbler Positioning System call (GPS).

Question: Chris, what do you do when a turkey comes in from an unexpected direction?

Answer: First of all, you can get out of position in a number of different ways. Although you set up with the perfect turkey hunt in mind, the turkey can do something to get you out of position. During opening day in New York, while you and I were hunting together, I heard a turkey gobbling in the tree. After I sat down, he flew down to the first ledge of the hill only 50 yards from the truck. When that turkey flew down to that ledge, he started gobbling. He strutted back and forth out on that ledge. We turned in the direction of the sound, and you pointed your gun to the bottom ledge. I didn't think the turkey would walk across the top ledge because the bird could spot the truck from there. I heard the gobbles and felt sure the turkey would show up on the first ledge an easy 25 yards from us. All of the sudden, you swung your gun 45 degrees to the left and pointed it at the crest of the hill. I said, "Can you see that turkey?" You replied, "Yeah, he's 35 yards from us. I moved my gun when the turkey was behind the tree, so he couldn't see me." I didn't have the heart to tell you that you spooked the turkey.

I tell everyone who gets out of position that when a gobbler comes in, wait and think before you move. Many times if you'll just wait, the gobbler will move right to where you want him to come. Think for five to ten seconds before you snap the gun over, make a quick movement or try to stand. Don't panic when things start to go wrong. Don't get overexcited. Don't do anything at all. Just sit there, wait, and let the turkey dictate your next move.

Natural Sounds Help Not Hurt

Question: What happens if you make a loud noise when repositioning?

Answer: Remain as quiet as you possibly can when you move through the woods. But don't think your hunt is over if you make a sound. Just remember you'll often hear that turkey come in to you before you see it. Natural sounds like leaves rustling and sticks breaking occur in the woods all the time. So when you snap a little limb or rustle some leaves, don't think the world ends at that point. That gobbler expects to hear some sort of sound as a hen comes to him, and calling just adds to the realism. If you have to make a move, do so softly, and give some yelps along with it. The gobbler will believe that a hen made that sound as she moved. Then he thinks, "Not only can I hear her calling, but now I can hear her walking toward me in the leaves."

Question: How do you know whether to move to a place where you can shoot or stay put and wait on the bird to dictate what to do?

Answer: You have to let the turkey dictate when you move and when you don't move. The terrain also dictates whether you can move or can't move. And to complicate it a little bit more, you have to match the mood of the turkey to the type of terrain you are hunting to know when to take the shot.

Later on in the morning, when you and I found three toms gobbling out in a field, we had to make the decision whether or not to move. We thought that the turkeys were still far enough over the crest of the hill in the field that we could move in close. The first time we set up, you couldn't see the edge of the field, so we thought the turkeys were still far enough out of range that you could move 5 or 6 yards to get a better shot. We thought that all I had to do was call the turkeys to the edge of the field so you could take one.

As the birds moved to you, a hawk flew above them. Instead of continuing to come down the edge of the field, all three gobblers dove into the thicket to get away from the hawk. Once the turkeys went into the thicket, I pointed my GPS call in their direction and followed through with the sound to the left to make the turkeys think that the hens were still there. I threw the call and the sound so that the gobblers would walk in front of you. I had initially started throwing it to the right, and as the turkeys moved to the right, I threw it back to the left. I kept in mind that in nature the hens go to the gobblers. So I just played hard to get. When I threw the call in a different direction, the gobblers changed directions to intercept the hen. I tried to throw the call to the other side so that the gobblers would walk in front of you. And when they did, you took a gobbler at less than ten steps. I really believe that by using a call that you can throw in different directions, you can better manipulate the gobbler as he comes in to you. This friction call allows you to make the hen sound come from any direction you choose and will actually enable you to move the gobbler to the spot you selected.

Using a Call to Move the Turkey

Question: How does the call move the turkey?

Answer: By turning the call around, you can make sounds like a hen walking around in a circle.

Question: Chris, when you have a turkey in close, and you know you are going to have to move to get off the shot, how do you know when to move, and how do you move through the woods?

Answer: If you can see the turkey, he can see you. So, wait until that turkey's head is hidden from you. Patience plays a big role. As soon as he spreads his tail feathers to you and his head is completely hidden, you can make a move on that turkey. He

If you can see the turkey, he can see you. Don't make
any abrupt moves when the turkey is in your view.
(Credit: John E. Phillips, Night Hawk Pub.)

may pick his head up if he hears a noise, but you want that head shot anyway. Wait to move until the gobbler goes behind a thick spot where he can't see you, or wait until the turkey puts his head completely behind the tree. Don't try to make a big, strong, abrupt move when that turkey is in full-face view of you. Let the turkey get as close as possible. If you need to make a big move, wait until he gets within 10 yards, then move the gun slowly and deliberately to get on that turkey. You have to remember that if you are in full Mossy Oak Camouflage, that turkey may not know what you are. And even though you've moved, he'll look hard at you before he breaks to run. Even if he does break to run, the turkey only will cover 10 to 30 yards of ground before he gets out of your gun range.

Avoid Snappy Movements

Question: If you have to make a move on a turkey, do you make a quick move or a slow move with the turkey looking at you? Most hunters want to throw the gun up quickly and get off the shot. When your gun is out of position, and you have to move it severely to the right or the left to have a shot at the turkey, what is the best way to make that move?

Answer: If you must make that move with the turkey in plain view, I suggest you move slowly and deliberately. While you make that slow and deliberate move, yelp at the same time

Move slowly and deliberately when a turkey comes into full view. The turkey will see the movement but won't recognize what he is seeing. (Credit: John E. Phillips, Night Hawk Pub.)

with a diaphragm call to confuse the bird. He'll often stay confused long enough for you to get off the shot. If you make slow and deliberate movements, the turkey will see that movement, but will not know what he is seeing. You will spook him a little bit, but if you try to snap shoot a turkey in full view of you, you will definitely spook him.

All types of predators attack turkeys. They get chased by coyotes and foxes, which sit in the thicket and pounce on them. So I believe when you make that snappy movement, they expect some type of predator to attack. Often, you can get away with just sighting in the gun on the turkey's head and making a good, clean kill. If the turkey is behind a tree, obviously, you can make that snap move without that turkey seeing you.

The Turkey That Sneaks up behind You

Question: When the turkey screams out his gobbles 10 yards behind you, what do you do?

Answer: When a gobbler screams right behind you at 10 yards, don't do anything at all. You can't see that turkey, but you can feel him breathing down the back of your neck. Sit still, and try not to breathe. Let that turkey walk off, then try to reposition and call him back in again to you. Nine times out of ten, if you attempt to make a move on a turkey that close, you'll just spook him. So, if a turkey is smart enough to come in behind you, let him walk off and call him in a different day.

Question: How much movement can you get away with?

Answer: You can't get away with any movement.

Question: What about noise and turkeys?

Answer: You can get away with some noise. You don't want to sound like a freight train coming through the woods, but a little rustle of the leaves helps. When a turkey comes in close, I like to take my hand and scratch softly in the leaves right beside me. You can bring in turkeys a little closer by scratching in the leaves. Leaf and twig noises are not bad sounds in the woods.

Sometimes they add a little bit of realism to what you want to accomplish.

Question: What about when you have to cough or clear your throat?

Answer: Don't.

Question: Do you cover it with a call?

Answer: You can cover a cough if you have a friction call. Try to run the call at the same time you cough, so that hopefully the call you make will mask your cough. But sometimes you still will spook high-pressured gobblers.

When a turkey takes you unprepared, you can draw him in closer by scratching in the leaves.
(Credit: John E. Phillips, Night Hawk Pub.)

9

Hunting Tight-Lipped Turkeys

By Todd Triplett

Todd Triplett is an avid outdoorsman who operates Wild Art Taxidermy and contributes regularly to outdoor publications such as North Carolina Game and Fish, Turkey Call, Carolina Adventure, *and* Tennessee Valley Outdoors. *He recently published* The Complete Guide to Turkey Taxidermy *with The Lyons Press. He lives in Lenoir, North Carolina.*

Nothing is more frustrating to the turkey hunter than a gobbler that won't respond to his best rendition of a lonely hen. Unfortunately this is often the case when birds have been heavily pressured by hunters, or that have an abundance of hens in the area. Another disadvantage that hunters face is trying to make the gobbler do something unnatural. Normally the hen goes to the tom. No matter the reasons that may cause a lock-jawed gobbler, the hunter who persists with varying tactics will eventually find success.

Some of my first attempts at turkeys were frustrating to say the least. After watching many videos and reading as much as possible, I assured myself the run and gun method was a sure bet. With not a bird to my credit, I knew this turkey business would be easy. The method was simple. Find a bird. Belt out a few loud and obnoxious calls and get the gun ready. So each of those first unsuccessful years I would venture out well before sunrise and listen for the first vocal bird. If I heard nothing, I would crow call sharply, wait a couple of minutes then find another spot. Most times by 9 A.M. I had exhausted all avenues and was headed home. If I did encounter a vocal bird I would find a comfortable spot and call. After a few minutes if a gobbler didn't come running to meet his demise I would once again be headed home. To say the least I was green to the ways of gobblers.

What follows are key tactics from myself as well as other respected turkey hunters who have harvested numerous birds and learned many lessons in the spring woods. Had the following information been available during my earlier turkey hunting attempts, I am sure a few more fans would hang on the wall.

Patience and Persistence

After a couple of fruitless seasons I became determined to take a gobbler. While on stand during deer season, I always seemed to see turkeys. From that observation, a plan was made. I would find an area that turkeys frequented, then I would wait while calling occasionally.

On a misty, early spring morning I put my plan into action. I found the perfect spot and settled in for a long wait. I made several pleas from a diaphragm, then remained motionless. My plan was to remain in one place and call every thirty minutes until lunch. My eagerness to hop from area to area was dimin-

The author enticed this gobbler with subtle and very limited calling.
(Credit: Todd Triplett)

ished as this was my last resort for success. I knew that if I sat long enough a gobbler would come.

And come they did. Within fifteen minutes I looked up the hill and saw a group of three gobblers silently headed in my direction. The birds hadn't made a sound but were definitely interested. Swiveling my position, I managed to point the smoothbore towards the threesome. After placing the bead on the lead bird, I squeezed the trigger. The sound of the blast still echoed from mountain to mountain as two of the three made a hasty getaway, leaving the third of their group flapping on the ground.

Had I used my previous tactic of "call and move," these birds would have found only a warm spot where I had been. But because I had opted to be patient, I had achieved success. Not long after that first successful hunt I managed to tag my second bird. Just as the first birds had come in silently so did the second, but this time it was nearly an hour before he showed. These experiences quickly taught me the virtue of patience.

Subtle Calling

David Gordon is a veteran turkey hunter who cut his teeth on mountain birds. One of Gordon's favorite tactics when dealing with silent birds is subtle calling. "If I know a bird is in the area that is reluctant to answer, I will position myself nearby and begin imitating the scratching of a turkey. This simulates a hen that is more interested in feeding than in breeding. Sometimes this is all it takes," says Gordon who has been pursuing North Carolina birds since 1983, a time when few others pursued this spring monarch.

Gordon will also add some very light calling while scratching. "Purrs and clucks that are almost inaudible can really entice a wary gobbler. Don't worry about calling too softly; a turkey's hearing is so keen it can hear the softest of sounds from long distances. And a lot of times if a gobbler hears what he thinks is a hen that isn't interested it will really fire him up. It seems to step on his ego," says Gordon.

Another key tactic that helps Gordon find frequent success is his willingness to commit to a bird. "Once I know a bird is somewhat interested, I will wait on him to make a mistake. Sometimes this may take a while, so I always carry a pair of pruning snips for cutting saplings to form a small blind," says Gordon. One of the toughest birds Gordon ever harvested came after setting up a similar blind and waiting for nearly two hours. "It was the middle of the day, which is one of my favorite times, and I heard a bird gobble. I quietly set up and begin to scratch and make the subtle sounds of a hen. The gobbler sounded off only three times in a two-hour period but I knew he was interested so I waited, being as motionless as possible," says Gordon. Once the wary bird felt things were safe, Gordon made a clean harvest. "I enjoy hunting wary birds; they are usually our best teachers," added Gordon.

Determine a Gobbler's Routine

William Terry, president of Legacy Premium Game Calls, says one of his most successful tactics for silent birds is to determine a particular bird's pattern. "Most turkeys will have a similar pattern from day to day. A bird will usually roost in a certain area. Then after leaving the roost, he will generally visit regular areas in search of hens. If a gobbler isn't vocal or willing to come to calling, the hunter has to determine those patterns if he is to be successful," says Terry, who has won the South Carolina State, senior division, turkey calling contest four times and the North Carolina Tarheel State, open division, once.

Too many times a hunter will set up on a gobbling bird in the morning to find nothing happens after flydown. Then they return the following morning only to encounter the same problem. Terry makes it a point to find out exactly where the bird went after leaving the roost. "If a gobbler flies down and continues to gobble as he walks away, his travel path is usually easy to determine. But if a bird only gobbles on the roost then doesn't gobble after flying down, I usually concentrate on his flapping wings and any other sounds that may let me know which direction he is going. After I am certain the gobbler has left the area I will move in and pick a likely spot along his travel route for the next morning. Usually I can harvest a bird in this situation within three days, says Terry.

Another favorite tactic of Terry's is what he dubbed "calling a bird away to you." Although this tactic may sound strange, it quickly makes sense to those who have encountered a wary gobbler that headed in the opposite direction once the pleading for company began. Terry said, "A lot of times a gobbler that has been pressured will respond well but will travel in the opposite direction of your calling. When this happens the gobbler has probably been bumped by another hunter. To combat this situation, a caller will set up where one would normally call from. Then in the direction the gobbler is likely to go, someone else will set up, remaining quiet. If the gobbler remains true to his previous pattern soon after flydown, he will be within range of the silent hunter. However if he decides that this morning is okay to go to the calling, the caller will take him. In this case someone should get an opportunity."

Reverse His Mood

"Make them respond," says Steve Puppe, public relations manager for Knight Muzzleloading. "If I encounter birds that aren't very vocal or seem to be hesitant to come in, I will sometimes call very aggressively. This is usually enough to excite even the most wary bird," says Puppe, who previously laid claim to nine state calling championships throughout the Midwest.

"Many times if a gobbler hears a deluge of hen talk he will think he is missing out on something exciting. Sometimes a hunter's calling is too timid. This usually works well for heavily pressured birds, but when it doesn't the hunter must change his strategy. I have called too many birds seductively and softly only to be turned down. Once my tempo and volume changed, so did the response I received," said Puppe.

Find His Strut Zone

According to long-time turkey hunter and outdoor writer Jim Casada, there are times when nothing will invoke a gobble from a wary bird. "Sometimes once a bird has been harassed or is with hens it will be reluctant to gobble on his own or respond to any calling. But there are several ways to find and take a bird in this situation. If you know an area holds birds, find a strutting zone and wait," says Casada.

Finding a bird's strutting zone can sometimes be tough. According to Casada, knowledge of the terrain is ideal. "If you are familiar with an area, you may already know of traditional strut areas. If not, start looking along ridge benches, logging roads and field edges. These are customary strutting areas. You will have to look carefully, but once a strutting zone is found the drag marks of the wings and possibly lost wing feathers will be evident. If you haven't disturbed the gobbler, he will likely show sometime during the day," said Casada.

But when the gobbler shows himself, the hunter best be prepared. According to Casada, a gobbler in this situation will almost always come in silent. "Usually a bird in this situation will slip in undetected as he meticulously scans his surroundings for trouble. If you move a hand or shift your position, the gobbler may leave without you even knowing he was there. The only way to combat this situation is to use a blind and remain still

One and one-quarter-inch spurs: a trophy in anyone's book.
(Credit: Todd Triplett)

until the moment of truth," said Casada. Other helpful tactics: Get as close as possible to the gobbler without being detected before calling. Use different calls—sometimes simply changing from a box to a slate will provoke a gobble. Put out decoys, preferably two hens and a jake.

Small Woodlots and Big Gobblers

Text and Photos By John Trout, Jr.

L ike many veteran turkey hunters, I first pursued turkeys in big timber. However, today many hunters find themselves chasing gobblers in small woodlots surrounded by agricultural fields. In fact, biologists and hunters have discovered this diverse habitat is extremely promising for expanding turkey flocks.

Take Hoosier National Forest in southern Indiana, one of the few areas in the state where you will find vast areas of hardwoods. I began hunting portions of the forest more than two decades ago. Recently, though, I've seen the birds flourish in small woodlots and farmlands surrounding the forest, as well as in woodlots around my home where there is no big timber for miles.

I've seen the same happen in Missouri. At one time, it seemed the vast timber areas of the Mark Twain National Forests provided most of the turkey hunting opportunities. Today, thanks to restocking programs and the turkey's adaptability, it's common to find large concentrations of birds in open agricultural areas.

Although it's no secret that you can find turkeys in small woodlots, don't assume you can hunt them the same way you do in big timber. Many hunters, including myself, believe these birds are the toughest of them all. You'll find your mistakes in this terrain are amplified, so avoiding errors must be part of your strategy.

Staying Invisible

Perhaps the biggest mistake you will make when hunting agricultural areas is getting spotted. I've learned the hard way that it's downright difficult to remain invisible when hunting small woodlots. Whenever you move to a bird, or just want to cross a field to get from one woods to another, there's a good chance a turkey will see you and vanish before you get to your spot. Moreover, it doesn't matter if you hunt flatlands or hills and hollows at dawn or during the day. However, you can take a few precautions to remain invisible.

Arriving early to listen for gobbles is standard turkey-hunting practice. But what you consider early in the big woods might be thirty minutes to an hour later than what I consider early in small woodlots. For instance, let's say you reach a listening point in the big woods fifteen minutes before gobbling begins. That might be fine if you're walking an old lane or parking your vehicle along a road in the middle of the dark timber.

But what if you have to cross an open field or park near a small woodlot? Keep in mind that even if it's dark, it will be lighter in the fields surrounding the woods.

In areas where I must cross an open field and walk a few minutes, I arrive about an hour before gobbling begins. The farther I need to walk, the earlier I arrive. That way, if I arouse the curiosity of a roosted bird because he spotted me, he might forget about me when the morning's first pink light triggers him to gobble.

I also stick to the low areas when moving, regardless of the time of day. Before dawn, after arriving at a listening point, I often wait until the birds are on the ground before moving closer. If I must cross one field to get to another after daylight, I stay in the valleys and avoid crossing over the top of a hill. When hunting the flatlands, I stick close to the fringes and fence lines when moving. However, you must decide for yourself whether it is better to move or stay put. This decision is easy once you know where the gobbler is.

Judging Distance

It's much easier to judge the distance between you and a gobbling bird if you hunt in big timber. Open areas, especially when it's windy, tend to reduce volume, often making a gobble sound farther away.

Many times, I've stood on the edge of a small woods only to hear a turkey near or in another woods across an open field. The biggest mistake a hunter makes in this situation is to move immediately toward the eager-sounding gobbler. Because the gobbler's volume is usually reduced, a hunter might think the turkey is on the other side of the woods when, in fact, he is along the fringe or just inside, where he could see you approach.

If you must cross an open field to get to a gobbler, first size up the situation. Distance is the primary consideration. If it's under 300 yards, it might be better to stop at the woods edge and call. Surprisingly, small-woodlot gobblers are not as reluctant as big-timber gobblers about crossing open areas.

Farmland Eastern gobblers spend much of their day feeding in and crossing fields, probably enjoying the security of being able to spot predators from a distance. Merriam's turkeys and

Three Eastern gobblers strutting across an open field.
(Credit: John Trout, Jr)

some Rio Grandes are known for their willingness to cross open country to get to a hen.

If terrain allows, I move across an open field. I believe it is better to stay where you are and try to get a gobbler to come than to spoil an opportunity by having a gobbler see you approach. If a gobbler is a quarter-mile or more away, you probably won't be able to lure him across a field. However, it might be possible for you to cut the distance by moving selectively in areas where you can stay hidden. Even if it means taking a longer route, it beats getting spotted.

Setups That Work

Naturally a large woods makes it easier to get in and work a gobbler without being spotted. However, gobblers in small woodlots are often closer to the fringes than they are to the center. For this reason, your approach to your setup is important.

It's a common practice to go straight to a gobbler. For example, let's say you are standing where a woodlot meets a field, and a turkey gobbles inside the woods about 300 yards to the south. The fringe runs north and south, so you could easily walk the edge to get even with the gobbler. After you are aligned, you could set up without penetrating deeply into the woods. Hunters often use this method, but it seldom offers the best opportunity.

When faced with the same situation, I use the field to my advantage and walk south to get closer to the gobbling bird, but only for a short distance. I might walk only 100 yards and set up along the fringe to make certain I won't be spotted. I also realize I will be silhouetted when moving along the fringe. You can decrease your chances of being spotted if you move only partway to the gobbler.

It also helps to choose a setup near the fringe in an area where the gobbler can get to you without a struggle. However, because the fringes of small woodlots are often thick, it might be impossible to do so. Because of this, many hunters will move even farther to look for the ideal setup. However, keep in mind that small-woodlot gobblers are not as reluctant as big-woods birds about moving through thick cover. I've seen them walk through seemingly impenetrable jungles of undergrowth to reach field edges.

Conversely, small-woodlot turkeys will consistently use pathways like old roadbeds and deer trails—when they are available—to get to fields. This habit makes agricultural gobblers easier to pattern than big-woods turkeys.

One area where my wife, Vikki, and I have set up consistently includes a major deer trail near the top of a hill. The trail comes out of the small woodlot and enters an agricultural field. It took a couple of years to learn that most of the turkeys came to the field at this location.

An Eastern gobbler strutting with a hen. (Credit: John Trout, Jr)

It's probably better to call turkeys toward fields than to call them from the fringe or field into the woods. Your calling will usually be met with gobbling but little else. After gobblers reach the fields, they prefer to stay there and strut as long as they don't spot you, or until the sun's warmth pushes them into the shade.

Because many gobblers will get to the field soon after leaving the roost, I prefer to select a listening point close to the fringe, or just inside the woods where I'm hidden. If a gobbler gets to the field and I must move to him, I avoid rounding a corner where I could be exposed. I'll set up just off the corner and attempt to lure the gobbler to my side of the field.

Decoy Pros and Cons

I seldom use decoys. The exception, however, is when hunting small woodlots early in the season. Decoys work well in agricultural areas, particularly when you must lure a distant gobbler across or along a field. However, decoys are also quick to fail when turkeys become familiar with them, which doesn't take long.

Just how long a decoy remains effective depends on several factors. I've had the best results during the first two or three days of the season. After that, the turkeys avoid approaching decoys, or skirt around them out of gun range. Keep in mind that a gobbler usually sees your decoys before he hits the field.

Mixing the number and types of decoys can help. For instance, early in the season, one hen decoy might be sufficient. However, if that fails, it might be necessary to add more decoys, including a jake, just to keep the birds guessing.

Nonetheless, when birds become decoy-shy, I leave the decoys in the vehicle. Surprisingly, a gobbler that might have refused to come to a decoy for a couple of days might be more likely to come to the call when he sees nothing.

Also, be aware that setting up decoys in a field makes you vulnerable. When you walk even a short distance into a field to set up or retrieve the decoy, you could be spotted.

Conclusion

I believe we have just started to scratch the surface when it comes to understanding hunting gobblers in and around small woodlots. We've discovered a few tactics that work well, but we'll probably learn more as hunters find themselves enjoying the unique challenges posed by small-woodlot turkeys.

Shotgun Willies

By Thomas McIntyre

Thomas McIntyre is the author of several books, including The Field & Stream Shooting Sports Handbook, Dreaming the Lion, *and* The Way of the Hunter. *He has written for* Field & Stream, Sports Afield, Gray's Sporting Journal *and* The Field. *His upcoming book,* Seasons and Days, *will be published by The Lyons Press in 2003. He lives in Sheridan, Wyoming.*

W hen was it that turkey hunters "lost their g—damn minds," to paraphrase gothic-redneck novelist Harry Crews?

At one time turkey hunting had a certain antebellum elegance—not the Old South charm of Scarlet and Tara, but more in the backwoods style of Boone and Crockett, or perhaps Pappy Yoakum. Mark Twain reminisced warmly (in what were the most cynical, bitter years of his late life) about the boyhood pleasures of hunting "the deceitful turkey," describing the art of it, in toto: "In the first faint gray of dawn the stately wild turkeys would be stalking around in great flocks, and ready to be sociable and answer invitations to come and converse with other excursionists of their kind. The hunter concealed himself and imitated the turkey-call by sucking the air through the leg-bone [sic] of a turkey which had previously answered a call like that and lived only just long enough to regret it." For his weapon, Twain took half-hour turns with his young cousin Fred in carrying "a small single-barrelled shotgun . . . not much heavier than a broom." And for a very long time that was about as solemnly as most southerners took their turkey hunting, while the rest of the Republic's citizens took it not solemnly, or even seriously, at all—for the plain fact that turkeys had been effectively extirpated in the rest of the Republic.

The great downfall of the simple art of turkey hunting came at the end of the twentieth and start of the twenty-first centuries, traceable to the unimagined triumph of wild turkey conservation, restoration, and transplantation. If classified as feathered big game (a definition I personally lean toward), the wild turkey would likely rank as the second most populous and widespread species in North America, right behind the whitetail and just ahead of the mule deer. What inevitably succeeds success, though, is excess. When turkey hunting expanded beyond its cult following in rural pockets below the Mason-Dixon Line to become a mass movement of continental proportions—even intercontinental with thriving wild populations in Hawaii, New Zealand, and New Caledonia, and reports of more turkey in Europe, Australia, and Africa—its commercial potential reared its ugly crimson-snooded head.

The first new products pitched to the *arriviste* class of wild turkey hunters weren't all bad. Better, more effective, more comfortable types and patterns of camouflaged clothing were welcomed. Turkey-hunting vests with padded seat cushions, and various types of low shooting stools, which helped hunters sit stiller, longer, were not to be sneered at. Maybe even decoys, to divert a bird's attention from the hunter, had a purpose (considering that the wild turkey sees more in a one-second glance than we can by "scanning the whole field [of view] piece by piece with the most accurate portion of [our] retina[s]," according to wildlife biologists). Those innovations had a reasonable fair-play intent: to try to deceive the wild turkey's most acute and developed sense, his vastly superior (to our own) eyesight, and draw him within the restricted range of a shotgun.

Unable to leave well enough alone, though, turkey-hunting-gear merchandisers kept looking for newer gadgets to market to a burgeoning cohort of turkey hunters, descending to a particularly ignominious nadir of hucksterism some years ago when one snake-oil peddler offered for sale a "cover scent" for turkey hunters, in spite of the fact that the wild turkey's brain lacks olfactory lobes of sufficient size to interpret smells—turkey are oblivious even to mothballs laid around the shelled corn they are attracted to by sight. This was on a par with promising that your blind would be better hidden by hanging a sign reading, "it's just a bush," on the outside of it.

As laughable as that may be, what has become of the turkey shotgun is not.

With human beings being human, and therefore toolmakers by disposition, there are always bound to be technological "improvements" in hunting weapons and ammunition. And in a hunting culture in which the blackpowder rifle, as just one example, has in a generation "advanced from nostalgic flintlock curiosity to in-line shotgun-primer ignition, jacketed-bullet-firing, not-even-black-but-smokeless-powder-loaded contraption," it would be naïve to believe that cartridge manufacturers, for instance, wouldn't start producing specialized turkey loads that were faster, heavier, and more tightly patterning than

Even 16-gauges will kill a turkey. (Credit: Thomas McIntyre)

conventional ammunition. Better ammunition does little, though, to tamper with the essential character of the turkey hunt (still fundamentally recognizable from Twain's description): The most sophisticated shotgun shell designed specifically for turkey doesn't shoot that much farther or kill more emphatically than any good-quality high-brass field load; the birds still have to be drawn into range.

The real madness with technology and turkey began when hunters started looking to their shotguns to extend the effectual outer limits of their lethality (yeah, sounds like a video game) beyond anything vaguely resembling traditional yardages. The first effort in this regard saw hunters lugging around behemoth 10-gauges. I bought into this idiocy myself for a brief but misguided interlude, hauling an 11-pound Spanish Laurona double with 32-inch barrels up and down hills, wearing myself out and being unable to hold the gun steady for more than a minute or two while in shooting position with a gobbler coming in. I put mine away after one too many missed turkey. (I know, Elmer Keith probably shot snipe with his 10-gauge double; alas, neither you nor I are Elmer Keith. The only really sensible use for a 10-gauge double that I ever heard was offered by Zimbabwean professional hunter Geoff Broom, who told me that he took the one he owned and sawed its barrels in half so he could feel somewhat comfortable about crawling into brushy thickets to shoot wounded leopard point-blank.)

Another and not entirely unreasonable option in the long-range game were varieties of extended screw-in choke tubes, dedicated to selected turkey-hunting loads. These made especial sense if you were shooting steel—required in some state and federal upland-hunting areas—or one of the other very effective nontoxic shot charges, whether Bismuth or Remington's Hevi-Shot; but they improved the patterning of lead shot, as well. They still didn't get you drastically out beyond regular ranges, though. So for some turkey hunters a tight choke, in and of itself, was not enough. Somewhere in the back of their minds there floated a charmed number, the mythic benchmark of turkey-hunting high performance, the grail: *The 50-yard shotgun.*

The most ardent attempt to capture this chimera was announced in a certain firearms company's 2002 press release attached to an e-mail (as you see, we're already some distance from *wing*bone calls, possibles bags, and buckskin moccasins). The release touted a "completely new concept in turkey barrel design," utilizing a bore with four stepped-down constrictions, going from overbore, to, like, really really tight. Further, the barrel was a "mid-weight target profile" that was "permanently affixed" to the receiver and "totally free floated," giving the shotgun *"the same treatment as a target rifle* [aghast italics mine]." The rif . . . shotgun had, naturally, a base for scope rings; and one writer who field-tested one—fitted out with a HOLOsight and shot from a bench and in a *vice*—lauded it for its ability to place 51 pellets of No. 5 short from a 3-inch 1⅝-oz, 12-gauge load at 25 yards (and 38 pellets at the magic 50 yards) in "what is considered the kill zone [his undefined words]."

Where to begin in analyzing this manner of . . . what? The term "outrage" springs to mind.

I never actually saw a picture of this wonder gun—and have slim ambition ever to lay hands on one—but I would make a money bet right here that by an impartial standard it's probably as fetching as a cow's posterior. Aesthetics aside, a number of critical technical aspects of the shotgun are not addressed in either the press release or the field test I read. What, for instance, does it weigh? What is the trigger pull like? How does it handle in actual hunting conditions and not on a bench and in a vice? Most important, will it kill turkey?

What matters most about any turkey shotgun, not just the one described above, isn't whether it offends our sensibilities, but how well it performs in the field. On the basis of pragmatism alone, there is good reason to be dubious about the merits of the entire modern school of (in all likelihood) very unwieldy target-rifle shotguns and the theory itself of wanting to assassinate turkeys at sniping distances.

In April of 2002, I *finally* took an Osceola turkey, completing my Grand Slam. I hunted with outfitter Jim Conley in Florida's Osceola county. Jim had taken his first turkey slam more than twenty years before, about the time he began outfitting; and with all his birds and all those he had guided hunters to, he had seen some five hundred turkey taken with shotguns. I had noticed him eyeballing my camo-ed, 12-gauge Remington Special Purpose 11–87 turkey gun when I took it out of its case. It has an extended choke for the 3-inch load of No. 5 Hevi-shot, a vent rib, and an orange "glow" front bead. Jim said he assumed I'd patterned it.

Sure, I said, which was the answer I usually gave my hygienist when asked about flossing. I *had* patterned it, sometime; I just couldn't quite recall when. Luckily, Jim got a 9-inch bearded tom to come into well within 30 yards, and I managed to center him with enough shot to drop him in a dry flapping of wings against the grass of the Florida pasture. As we carried the gobbler from the field, Jim explained why in recent years he had gotten chary about his hunters' weapons of choice.

Jim could not remember any hunter he guided ever missing a turkey—until big 10s and extreme turkey chokes began appearing on the scene. With the 10-gauges in particular he started seeing a mounting number of misses and cripples. The reasons why were clear to him: The guns, first, kicked—hard (they are shot, remember, generally when a hunter is seated, leaning against a tree, with nowhere for the recoil to go but right into the hunter's shoulder), cultivating devastating flinches in their owners. If you wanted them to recoil less, you had to make them weigh so much that you needed a gun carriage to move them around the field, and it was almost impossible to hold them steady for the lengthy periods required to get a gobbler in close and in position with his head out. And shotgun triggers were never engineered to be the sort of precision instruments that the triggers of target rifles were. The main problem, though, was that turkey hunters wanted those 10s and specialist 12s to be, you guessed it, 50-yard guns!

For Jim, 50 yards was a far from "appropriate" range for trying to kill turkey. At that distance, the front bead of a shotgun would almost entirely obscure a gobbler's head, making an accu-

Superguns are not needed in close-range kills.
(Credit: Thomas McIntyre)

rate shot problematic at best. (Wouldn't that make a turkey scope a possible solution? Not as much as might be thought, as we will see.) At the same time, there *is* such a thing as a turkey coming in too close—it's no mean feat to hit the bouncing ball of a turkey's head when it's only feet away and the pattern that the shotgun is throwing is the metaphorical diameter of a soda straw. Jim's conclusion was that the wonder guns were more trouble than they were worth, prone more to underkill (and misses) than to overkill. Shotguns were made to *point*, not aim, at turkey at reasonable ranges; and any gun that patterned well (and that you actually *had* patterned), loaded with a suitable cartridge and of an adequate gauge, would work just fine. And sometimes even what constituted an "adequate" gauge was open to debate.

I was Jim's last hunter in Florida for the season, and a couple of weeks later, he was out in Texas, patterning a .410 Mossberg pump—vent rib, single bead—on a 30-yard plywood target. The gun's 3-inch shell put enough of its ⅞ oz.-load of No. 6 pellets deep enough into the board for Jim to carry it with him when he went out for Rio Grande turkey. He'd preached against the wretched excesses of wonder guns for so long that it was time to verify for himself that what counted when it came to killing turkey was "not the size of the load you shoot," but "where you put the shot." The .410 turned out to be "light and steady to hold" (not to mention a joy to walk with), had "no recoil and very little noise," and bagged a Lone Star gobbler for him cleanly at 27 paces, which is considered a conservative distance.

Using a .410 might be an immoderate way of proving a point, but there is nothing remotely moderate about hunting turkey with a 10- or tricked-out 12-gauge with a scope and a choke like a high-pressure hose nozzle. If I had been carrying guns like that, I doubt I would have taken either of the big Merriam'ses I killed on the same late-spring Sunday in 2002.

I hunted outside the tiny (kind of a redundancy) northwest South Dakota town of Bison with writer-photographer Mark Kayser and with John De Palma of C.C. Filson Company. (The hunt also provided an opportunity to put some of Filson's new wool Advantage Timber camo clothing to work, and it performed well in the cool, sometimes drizzly, air.) Where we hunted, among the cottonwood creek bottoms of a large ranch, was in a two-bird area.

The first of those two birds that we spotted was at mid-morning on the far side of a creek bottom, "stalking" around with his flock. We moved down the creek so the turkey wouldn't see us drop into it, and worked our way back, through the mud-holes, fallen cottonwoods, turkey feathers, and turkey droppings. We set up twice, putting out decoys, and tried to call the gobbler to us. He answered our calls, but would not come down into the bottom. Then we heard him going away.

We ended up crawling after him to where he was gobbling below us at the bottom of a steep bank. Mark wormed to the edge and yelped, holding up a jake decoy. Infuriated, the gobbler came, spitting and drumming, up the bank and onto the flat where we were proned out, trying to press ourselves into invisibility in the dry prairie grass. As the gobbler strutted toward us, the hens he had with him came up, too, and bustled past, forming a phalanx between him and what they took to be a foreign hen. The gobbler broke strut and ran to catch up with them. Now we were covered up in turkey, none of them more than 15 paces away. There was only time for me to roll to my side and cant the 11–87 up so I could find the orange bead at the end of the rib and the gobbler's tall red head just beyond it. This was when a scope would have been literally worse than useless—I doubt even a rear sight, admittedly useful for keeping a turkey-hunter's head down on the gun, would have done any good. Lined up on the 20-pound turkey, I slapped the trigger and there was a sirocco of beating wings and whirling feathers, the rest of the flock scurrying away out the yellow ridges and draws.

After lunch, we went off in the direction the rest of the flock had taken, and this time—maybe wanting to verify something to myself—I switched out the "special purpose" turkey shotgun for a blued 16-gauge Ithaca Model 37 with a 26-inch vent-rib, full-choke barrel with a white bead at the muzzle. And instead of a magnum turkey shell, I pumped into the chamber a high-brass 2¾-inch cartridge loaded with 1⅛ ounces of No. 6 shot.

We followed the draw we had seen the birds heading up in the morning and climbed the slope of a bald knob, easing forward as we neared the crest. Almost to the top, we saw three nearby jakes trotting off to our left, having come out of the draw on the other side of the knob. We dropped to our bellies, and Mark *moo*-ed to reassure the jakes that we were innocuous bovines. The jakes went off, and from the draw ahead of us came a gobble.

Mark got out the fatal jake decoy again, and we wriggled up to where we could see down into the draw. Mark yelped. A single boss gobbler strutted behind an oak at something very close to 50 yards away. His tail was spread, and he turned back and forth like a piñata begging to be hit. When his head went behind the oak, I got the 16-gauge up and waited for him to come out from behind the tree. Again, if I'd had a scope—mounted on a 12-gauge—I would probably have a shot; but I couldn't have guaranteed that I would have killed. The gun I had, though, simply precluded that option, and left me with what was the only correct one: to wait.

A second tom gobbled 200 yards from us, answering Mark's yelp. Two hens were with the boss gobbler below, and they drew him away now from what they believed was the sound of a rival. Going with them, the dominant tom veered toward the approaching one and ran him around in a pro forma display of superior rank, before returning to the females and wandering away. The second gobbler tolerated the abuse, because the field had been cleared for him to come after the inviting female he believed was on the knob, and he was coming fast.

Mark and I rolled and slid off the back of the knob and dropped into the wash below, quickly putting out the jake and two hen decoys and lying up off to the side and in front of the decoys in the shade of a deadfall cottonwood. I had the lightweight shotgun up and resting comfortably on my knees. Mark gave one more yelp and within a minute I heard drumming and spitting, then saw the white rim of a fanned tail skylined at the crest of the knob. I waited for the bird to come all the way over the crest, so his entire body was on our side, and he couldn't duck back. It didn't matter; he was committed to coming all the way.

A dozen yards above us on the slope, his attention focused on the decoys, the turkey drew himself up, thrust his neck forward, and gobbled almost in our masked faces. I pushed off the safety and pressed the trigger, and without benefit of optics, magnum turkey-load, high-tech choke, or target-rifle "treatment," killed the 18-pound bird as dead as if he were a cottontail, deader if possible than I'd killed the bigger bird earlier in the day.

Which is to say that the simple art of turkey hunting is, at heart, about knowing turkey country and turkey habits, and using that knowledge to bring wild turkey close enough to kill them cleanly with a shotgun meant for pointing, not aiming. If you want to complicate matters by hunting turkey with a rifle (there are several states in which it is legal), use a rifle: It takes no small measure of competent marksmanship to kill a wild turkey with one, and not end up with something that looks like it was scraped off a highway. On the other hand, you shoot a turkey at long range with a rifle, at least it's going to be dead—an outcome not at all preordained when you try to "stretch the barrel" on a shotgun.

In the end, though, if you absolutely cannot get through life without a wonder turkey gun, then by all means buy one. I'm sure it'll look swell beside all those bottles of turkey cover scent you bought, way back when.

Location is Everything

By Gary Clancy

Gary Clancy has written for most of the major outdoor magazines, and is a book author, photographer, and hunting seminar speaker. His book, Treestand Hunting Strategies, *was published by The Lyons Press in 2002. He hails from Byron, Minnesota.*

I met Eddie Salter on a moonless, darker-than-the-inside-of-a-cat night many years ago when he picked me up at the Montgomery airport and whisked me away to his turkey camp. We were talking away—actually, I was talking, Eddie was drawling—as hunters do, when suddenly Eddie put on the brakes and pulled off to the side of the gravel road. I thought the coffee we had been drinking had finally got to Eddie, but Eddie had not stopped to answer nature's call.

"There's a bird been roosting on this little ridge some," Eddie drawled. "Let's just see if he's at home." Eddie got out of the truck, put his right hand to his mouth and cut loose with an old-fashioned "who-cooks-for-you?" owl hoot. A gobbler came right back. "Yup, thought he might be here," Eddie said and slid back into the truck.

Now I've never considered myself the suspicious type, but then I'm not naïve either. Maybe, just maybe, I thought, this fine southern gentleman was trying to set up this Yankee writer with a bird which if not an actual pet, could easily be described as ultra-dependable. But then Eddie put my suspicions to rest. A half-mile down the road from where he had owl hooted the first time, he stopped again, hooted once and got another reply. Before we finally rolled into camp, Eddie had located four gobblers with his middle-of-the-night owl hooting. Getting on a bird a couple of short hours later in the morning was a piece of cake.

As in Real Estate, . . .

Location is everything when it comes to turkey hunting. Sure, turkey sign such as scratching and droppings are indicators that birds are in the area, but nothing beats actually hearing that old gobbler roll out across the timber. Very simply, if you can't locate gobblers, you darn sure can't kill one. That is why most of the top-notch turkey hunters I know place major emphasis on locating tactics. These hunters know that the best calling in the world will be to no avail if there is not a gobbler within hearing distance of that call. Just as a pro fisherman might spend several hours looking for fish before actually fishing for them, the best turkey hunter I know will go all out to locate a bird before actually setting up for serious calling. A mistake many of us make is to pick a spot that simply looks good, get all set up and start trying to call birds to us. Although this tactic can be successful at times, a far better use of the precious hours we have to be afield is to first locate the gobbler and then go to work on him.

Of Owls, Crows and Coyotes

No two hunters have the same ideas when it comes to locating turkeys. Eddie Salter, for instance, likes to let the morning build on its own and let the gobblers go ahead and gobble if they are going to. But if it gets light enough that the first crow of the morning sounds off and he still has not heard a gobble, Eddie will go to work owling.

An accomplished mouth caller, Eddie sounds so much like a barred owl that several times while hunting with him we had live owls come swooping in to land in the trees around us. I suspect that whatever Eddie says in owl languages is X-rated, and turkey season being also the mating period for the barred owl, the male owls are anxious to converse with Eddie. But as Eddie sees it, all of that owl activity can be a handicap for the turkey hunter.

"You get down into a swamp where the owls like to hang out, and when the mating season is on, you can bet those owls have been tearing it up all night long. Any turkey roosted in the vicinity is sick of listening to owls hooting and unlikely to respond to an owl call no matter how good it sounds," says Eddie. "But before I give up on the owl hooting, I always try a reed-type call like my Screaming Owl. I designed this call for volume and high pitch, and many times I'll get a bird to gobble with the Screaming Owl call that ignored my best attempts at mouth calling."

Even though Eddie usually depends upon owling to locate birds in the early morning hours, he admits that there are places where owling just doesn't work worth a hoot (pardon my pun). "Maybe it's because there are too many owls in a certain place and the birds are so accustomed to hearing them that they don't gobble to an owl, or maybe it's the other way around, I really don't know," confides Eddie. "But I do know that there are places in this country where it is rare to get a bird to gobble at an owl hoot. But a crow call will work anywhere I've ever hunted."

Eddie Salter woos gobblers with various mouth calls.
(Credit: Gary Clancy)

When hunting in the western states, Eddie relies heavily on a coyote howl to locate birds, and as a last resort he uses the coyote howl even in the East where coyotes are less plentiful.

Tricks, Tried and True

Mossy Oak's Ronnie "Cuz" Strickland once said about Eddie, "The man honestly believes that there is a gobbler behind every tree." What Cuz meant was that if Eddie feels he is in good turkey country, he knows that there is likely a gobbler within hearing distance at any given time. That's why Eddie pulls out all of the stops when it comes to locating.

"One time I could not get turkeys to respond to any of my calls—owl, crow, coyote, nothing. But then this boat came up a nearby river on a real misty morning and blew its fog horn. Well, that timber just lit up with gobbling turkeys. Next morning I had me one of the portable, handheld fog horns in my hunting vest."

Then there was the time hunting Rios in Texas that Eddie noticed that the gobblers were responding to a bellowing, old Brahman bull. Eddie started imitating the half-mad, half-sad bellow of a bull, which had been fenced off from its cows, and those Rios went nuts.

"I'll even go with a gobble as a last resort," says Eddie, "but only if I'm pretty darn sure that there are no other hunters on the property. Gobbling is a sure way to bring in other hunters, which can not only goof up the hunt but can be potentially dangerous. But if I'm hunting where I'm sure I'm alone and nothing else is working, a gobble is a good way to get some action going in the morning. Seems like sometimes every gobbler in the woods is just waiting for that first one to open its beak, then they all start in.

Cutting and Running

Like most good turkey hunters, Eddie does a lot of loud cutting during the day in an effort to prompt a gobble. On quiet days in open timber, Eddie relies mainly on a diaphragm call, but in heavy timber or when the wind is blowing Eddie goes with his Old Master box call.

Eddie's style of cutting is a bit different from most in that he likes to mix up his cutting with some very loud and aggressive yelps. Many times a turkey will gobble just as Eddie drops off the cutting and throws in a few of those excited yelps.

Nothing beats a good box call. Here Salter moves the box call around to increase its range. (Credit: Gary Clancy)

When you need to really reach out and touch them, nothing will beat a good box call. And you can really increase the range of your box call by pointing the sound chamber (the hollow portion of the box) in the direction you want the sound to go. Eddie often moves his box call around like some kind of radar dish, in effect throwing the sound wherever he points the call. It works for Eddie Salter, and it will work for you.

This spring remember: Just as is true in real estate, when it comes to spring turkey hunting, location (and locating) is everything.

Offbeat Tactics for Bad Birds

By Jim Casada

"Some men are mere hunters; others are turkey hunters." Thus did Archibald Rutledge, a beloved Southern sporting scribe of yesteryear, describe those who have become hopelessly enamored of His Majesty, the wild gobbler. As Rutledge and countless others of his ilk readily recognize, turkey hunters are truly a breed apart. They threaten marital harmony for months prior to the opening of the spring season while "talking turkey" as they practice their calling skills. The season, which blessedly lasts a month or less in most states, finds them veritable zombies—rising long before daylight to be afield and "setup" at false dawn, and even their shortened spans of sleep are troubled as dreams of what might have been and replays of error-filled outings course through the hunter's mind.

Most of all though, turkey hunters revel in misery. Failures are an integral part of the sport's folklore, and those devoted to the uneven quest for lordly gobblers delight in sharing tales of their misfortunes, miscues, and missed shots. Most of all though, old masters of the rites of spring love to cuss and discuss what are often called "bad birds." These are particularly troublesome toms, gobblers which have, for one reason or another, repeatedly outwitted hunters and sent them home empty-handed. To match wits with such a turkey is an exercise in delight; to win such a contest, maybe because it so seldom happens, is sheer ecstasy. What follows is a sort of primer on bad birds, with guidance being offered by noted hunters who have known ample tribulation and occasional triumph in their dealings with the savvy sultans of spring.

Many of their tactics are offbeat or downright unorthodox, but in the scenarios which follow, chances are you will recognize a situation or two similar to ones you have encountered over the years. If so, here are how the experts have dealt with bad birds, and their advice should give you some grist for your mental mill in your own dealings with the elusive elite among America's greatest gamebird.

Hung up Birds

One of the most commonly encountered difficulties with savvy turkeys is toms that, in the sport's parlance, "hang up." Bob Walker, a highly successful competition caller and longtime guide at Bent Creek Lodge in Alabama, has had more than his fair share of dealings with such turkeys. "These turkeys get hunted and hunted hard, day after day," Walker says, "and as a result the survivors get mighty suspicious. They will respond to a call, but it sometimes seems like they have a mindset which says only so far and no further. When that happens, with the

Bob Walker in calling mode. (Credit: Jim Casada)

bird being reluctant to come closer than 100 yards or so, I have found two tactics that work well.

"The first is creating what I like to think of as a 'comfort level' for the gobbler. I do this by scratching in the leaves. A lot of folks know this approach, but they make a mistake by rustling leaves a few times then stopping. Turkeys, when they are feeding, are constantly walking and scratching, and you need to do the same thing. Often doing that, as opposed to calling, will bring a reluctant gobbler within gun range."

A second tactic which Walker recommends is quite different in nature. "When I have been working a bird for some time," he says, "especially one which responds readily to yelping without coming on in, I try to take the game to him. I'll yelp really hard or maybe do a bit of cutting, then I'll move up as much as I dare. You've got to know your terrain to do this, because obviously this isn't possible in places like wide-open swamp bottoms. Once I've moved, I won't call any more. I'm convinced that gobblers sometimes gobble to get the hen to yelp, and when he doesn't hear the hen, curiosity can work in your favor." Obviously this is a tactic which can be employed only with birds which gobble lustily, but any hunter with much experience can think back on times when he could make a turkey gobble almost at will yet failed to kill him. Walker's "move and hush" approach might just have been the ticket to success.

Patterning Problem Turkeys

Preston Pittman has devoted much of his life to turkey hunting, and he is an individual who actually delights in dealing with difficult gobblers. His favorite approach to such situations relies on research and reconnoitering as opposed to calling.

"I ask myself a number of questions," Pittman says. "What is the turkey doing? Why is he doing it? When is he doing it?" Once Pittman has what he feels is a reasonable set of answers to such questions, along with a full understanding of the terrain, he is ready to put the information he has compiled to use. "Time is probably the key factor in dealing with wise, wary turkeys," he maintains. "A lot of folks simply aren't willing to pay the necessary price in terms of patience, but for me the ultimate rewards are well worth the effort."

Preston Pittman with a "bad" turkey. (Credit: Jim Casada)

To that end, Pittman says that the worst mistake you can make is aggressive calling. "Everyone likes to hammer birds and listen to the sound of their own calling," he notes, "but that is not the way to deal with bad turkeys." Instead, Pittman makes it a point to do relatively little calling in such situations, and what he does is soft. "I like the soft sounds which are customary for turkeys as they go about their everyday activities," he says. "Clucks, purrs, whines, and pips, as opposed to loud yelping, are the way to a wise old gobbler's heart."

Dealing with "Henned up" Pasture Birds

One of the most common difficulties hunters face with gobblers, and it is one which gets a lot of toms dubbed as "bad" when they really are not, is dealing with a bird accompanied by a bevy of hens. This is doubly difficult when the group is regularly using a pasture or open fields, because they have no reason or inclination to leave safe, comfortable surroundings. Often gobblers in such situations respond to calls readily and regularly, but the message they are sending is, in effect, "you are welcome to join the party, but it is over here, not where you are."

When asked about such situations, Mark Drury, the owner of M.A.D. Calls and a renowned contest calling personality, laughingly said: "The best way to deal with 'henned up' toms in a pasture is with a rifle." Then, in a more serious vein, he turned to an approach he has used successfully in such situations. "I apply old-time fall scattering tactics to spring hunting," he says. "If you can break up a gobbler and his harem by disrupting their routine, the situation changes suddenly and dramatically.

"What I do is try to get as close as possible to the group of turkeys, then rush them, making sure to note which way the tom flies as I do so. If some of the hens take the same route, I'll course them and follow up with a secondary scatter. Then I just set up in the general vicinity of where the gobbler went. Often he will begin gobbling on his own after things settle down, which usually takes an hour or maybe a bit longer, but if that doesn't happen I will begin doing some soft yelping when I feel the scare from the scatter has been forgotten.

"A gobbler which has become accustomed to female company can get lonely in a hurry, and when you get him alone a lot of positive things can happen." Drury also notes that another facet of the scattering situation is to determine where the birds roost and then break up the flock while they are still in the trees. "You can do this in the evening or at daylight, although I prefer the former. If hens start converging on the gobbler at daylight when he sounds off, just run them away. Sometimes under these circumstances a tom which has seemed impossible suddenly becomes highly responsive."

The Realities of Dealing with Roosted Birds

Wilbur Primos, a leading callmaker and lifelong turkey hunter, has found that difficult turkeys which have been roosted require some special considerations. "While standard wisdom holds that you should get as close to a roosted bird as possible without spooking him," Primos says, "I don't think that always holds true. When you get in really tight the gobbler naturally expects the hen to come to him. On the other hand, if the distance is somewhat greater, he may come to the conclusion that he has to make a commitment.

"A good example came with a bird I hunted a few years back for two straight weeks. I was able to get close to him on the roost day after day, only to have him leave me once he flew down. Finally, I set up 200 yards away and did not do any calling until I thought he was on the ground. He came to me because I forced him to make a move."

What Primos had done was to back off, and he adds that "backing up may be one of the best ways to kill a tough turkey. It just seems to me, and I base this on a lot of experience," he says, "that when you are really close a gobbler feels it is only reasonable for you to come to him. When the distance is greater though, I have found that if you can get his attention enough

Will Primos plays it cautiously with little or no calling.
(Credit: Jim Casada)

to get a commitment, then play it cautiously with little or no calling, that often the bird will come on in. Or, if you want to put it that way, don't go by the book when dealing with a difficult tom."

The Delights of Double Teaming

Chris Kirby, who handles public relations for Quaker Boy Calls along with being one of the most successful competitive callers of recent years, has had considerable success employing two-man tactics, with a decoy and some of the same sort of backing up Primos advocates. "A few years back in New York a buddy and I locked horns with a gobbler who would come within 80 yards but no closer. This was the case even though we were using a decoy which he clearly saw on more than one occasion.

"Eventually I used a variant on the old two-man approach where one hunter awaits the tom while the other backs away and calls. As soon as we got the bird to gobble, my friend set up with the decoy some 50 yards *behind* him and with me another 50 to 60 yards back. I called from that position and this time the shy gobbler's 80-yard safety zone didn't do him any good. Since that time, I've used a similar approach with good results on several other occasions. It is sort of double-teaming toms with a different twist."

Obviously the suggestions of these experts do not cover all the bases, and each of them made a point of emphasizing the fact that "bad birds" get dubbed as such because they make a habit of defeating the best efforts of hunters. Still, these sportsmen have found that by using their wits, along with an ample measure of patience, persistence, and willingness to try the untried, they can periodically emerge from the greening up woods of spring triumphant. Such triumphs are especially sweet, and by adopting and adapting their suggestions to your own hunting situations, you may share the undeniable joys to be derived from coming to a successful match point with a troublesome tom.

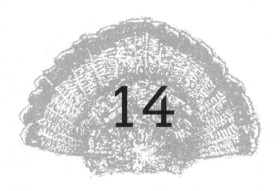

Gobblers under the Weather

By Gerald Almy

Gerald Almy has been a full-time outdoor writer for nearly thirty years, with two books and several thousand magazine articles for over one hundred publications to his name. He was a staff writer for Sports Afield *magazine for nineteen years and hunts and fishes throughout North America. Gerald has hunted turkeys in more than a dozen states. He lives in the Shenandoah Valley of Virginia with his wife and daughter.*

The air is crisp but not too cold. There's just a hint of wind, the sun is shining brightly—few are the gobbler hunters who have experienced such perfect conditions. A typical spring turkey hunt usually features sleet, rain, snow, fog, lightning, extreme cold, scorching heat, relentless wind or some witches' brew of these unfavorable conditions. At least that's the way it has been for me in more than twenty years of spring gobbler hunting in over a dozen states. Some of the more memorable extremes I've faced include 50-mph winds in New York, 105-degree F heat in Texas and 2 feet of snow in Nebraska's pine hills.

But you learn to cope. What else can you do when your day off comes at a certain time or when the trip you've planned for months finally arrives—and the weather is bad? I've learned over time that poor conditions don't necessarily ruin the hunt. You just have to learn to deal with it head-on by analyzing the negative conditions and determining how to adjust your gear, location and strategy.

Bagging a gobbler is the ultimate goal, of course, but even in the best of circumstances, no one can expect to kill a turkey every time out. By adjusting to the environmental conditions at hand, however, you can often work birds even in the most miserable weather. As a bonus, most other hunters usually sleep in or stay at camp on these days, so you often have large tracts of woodlands all to yourself. And at times the birds will oblige you even further by coming into clean shotgun range.

Rain

A mist or light sprinkle often has little effect on toms, and the damp woods actually help you make a quiet approach into good calling range. If you wear glasses, make sure you have a hat with a brim to keep raindrops off. Keep slate and box calls in an inner pocket until the rain stops. Glass and mouth calls are best used during precipitation.

Quality raingear will help you stay comfortable and dry in these and even heavier downpours. If you don't own one of the new quiet, laminated types of raingear, wear a light wool, cotton or fleece jacket or shirt over the top of your rain jacket to stay silent when you move through brush. Most raingear is simply too loud to wear in the turkey woods.

Avoid calls such as box or slate in wet weather—use mouth calls instead. (Credit: Gerald A. Almy)

Turkeys rarely come down off their roosts in very hard rain, so if it's pouring down right at first light, the wisest course of action is to hold off and hope for a break. This requires discipline when you really want to be out turkey hunting, but it's more prudent than going out and potentially spooking birds that would likely come in to your calls if you were a bit more patient.

If you wait an hour or two or even until as late as 10 or 11 A.M., the heaviest rain may slack off and the birds will fly down, eager to find companionship. If the weather completely changes and the sun starts to break through at this time, gobblers often become extremely vocal after having stayed on the roost so long.

Stay close enough to hunting territory to be in good gobbler territory the minute skies lighten. The hunting then is often even better than at first light.

Turkeys don't like to brush their feathers against wet bushes or saplings during the rain. If the birds are already off the roost when it starts to pour, they often take cover in conifer stands with an open understory. Sometimes they'll move out into fields, where their oily feathers allow moisture to bead up and roll off. Even if they do stay in timber during the rain, the first place gobblers head to as the showers ease is a field, meadow or open logging road, where they can shake off the moisture and spread their feathers to dry in the sunlight. Hit such locations during or immediately after a rain and call from the edge of the woods, or try to spot the birds first and then call. If no toms are present, move on to the next field.

Thunder and Lightning

Thunderstorms are often short-lived in spring, and far from shutting down turkey activity, rumbling clouds often stimulate gobblers to call. Move to a safe place—away from tall trees but not exposed in a field. Put your gun down a short distance away. If you're in camp or your vehicle, listen for gobbling birds during the thunderstorm, then move to them as soon as the hard downpour and lightning stop.

Hunting in a thunderstorm is a balancing game. Never let your desire to duel with a gobbler outweigh safety considerations. If the storm is bad, seek shelter and wait it out. In the right situation, however, a quick-moving thunderstorm can actually cause turkeys that would otherwise have remained silent to gobble. When the rain stops, you can move in and work them. Some of these birds may sneak in silently, but because you'll know they are there, you'll have the confidence to keep calling even if they don't gobble as they slink in.

Snow

The effect of snow on turkeys varies with the location. In southern areas, where snow isn't common, a dusting can shut down gobbling and turn birds off. In the West, Midwest and Northeast, where snows in spring season aren't rare, a few inches will have little effect on the birds.

A hunt in Nebraska when over a foot of snow fell.
(Credit: Gerald A. Almy)

A heavy snowstorm, however, will shut down birds no matter where you're hunting. Even if they still want to chase hens, it's not possible with the deep snow. I was hunting the pine hills of Nebraska when 24 inches of snow fell during the second day of the hunt. I actually elicited a gobble from the porch of the lodge, but it was just wishful thinking on the bird's part. We drove, walked, and called all day, but we didn't even see a track. I don't believe a single bird flew out of a tree until the snow began to melt the next day.

If you hit a blizzard like that one, it's best simply to head home and plan to hunt another time. But if the snow is only a light or moderate one, move, if possible, to lower areas—nearby valleys or lowlands with gentler weather. They might have less snow or none at all. Look to southern exposures, where the snow will generally accumulate more slowly and warm more quickly than in other areas.

Often birds will roost in conifers during snowfalls, so hunting near these areas is a good bet. After the snow stops falling and birds resume their activities, look for fresh tracks and determine their direction.

Sleet

Sleet is worse than a hard rain or light snow. Gobblers don't like to venture out in it and usually remain on the roost, where evergreens often protect them somewhat from the icy downpour. Wait it out, then be ready to move into position as soon as the inclement weather breaks. Fields, old logging roads or hardwoods near conifer stands are good bets right after a sleet storm breaks.

Wind

Strong, pummeling winds may well be the most common bad weather experienced by spring turkey hunters. It robs you of your ability to hear birds unless they're very close, and it prevents gobblers from hearing your calls as well. One tactic I like to use when heavy winds are predicted is simply to move in quickly on birds I've roosted the night before or located at first light, hoping to call one in before the wind grows stronger, as it often does later in the morning.

If you don't score early, plan on covering a lot of territory to locate a bird willing to talk in spite of the wind. Call often and loudly. Boxes, tubes and wingbones can be heard for long distances. Set up fast when you hear a tom in such conditions, because he's probably close.

Another useful strategy for windy days is simply to go where the wind isn't too strong. By searching out coulees, valleys, secluded hollows and the lee sides of hills and mountains, you can often find hidden pockets of terrain where barely a breeze is stirring. Gobblers often move to these protected areas so they can be heard by hens and escape the flapping shrubbery and rattling branches that rob them of their ability to hear predators.

Bitter Cold

This really doesn't affect turkeys as much as many hunters think. Turkeys are extremely hardy, and I've called in toms on days when temperatures didn't leave the teens. Southern birds, however, do tend to be a bit close-mouthed after a cold front lashes in. The best solution then is to hunt during late morning and afternoon (where legal), when the toms have warmed up a bit. Also, be alert for birds slinking in silently on frigid mornings.

Extreme Heat

This can occur anywhere that turkeys are hunted, particularly late in the season. On days when temperatures approach the 100-degree F mark, toms seem more concerned with staying cool and finding plenty to drink than they do with mating. However, there is usually a burst of calling and mating activity right at dawn. That's the time to move fast, setting up tight to birds even at the risk of spooking them. You want to get a gobbler coming to you before the sun completely rises over the horizon.

If you don't score early, look to shaded draws, stream bottoms and areas with springs or ponds. Toms will head to these areas within a few hours of sunrise to obtain moisture and retreat from the heat of open, sun-baked areas. Call sparingly in these locations, because the birds will likely be heading for them anyway and you don't want to risk alarming them. If the terrain is open enough, these are excellent spots for placing a decoy near the water source.

Hunting near water may help in extreme heat.
(Credit: Gerald A. Almy)

Fog

Fog isn't as bad as it might seem. Birds often gobble well in fog, and it has tactical advantages. Since toms can't see as far, they are less likely to hang up out of range. By the time they get to where they feel they should see a hen in these murky conditions, they're often within shotgun range. Fog dampens the forest floor, too, allowing you to move quietly into close calling range.

The main drawback of fog is that *you* can't see as well or as far—and neither can anyone else. That could allow another hunter to approach dangerously close without your realizing it. With hunters making turkey sounds while wearing total camouflage, the potential for an overeager hunter to *think* he sees a bird when he spots movement increases.

On foggy days, try to avoid areas where other people are likely to be. Wear a fluorescent orange hat and/or vest when moving through the woods, also refrain from calling while you are moving.

15

Woods Wise Turkey

Gary Sefton's Ten Secrets for Using a Box Call

By John Phillips

I joined Gary Sefton, promotions manager at Woods Wise Products, in Franklin, Tennessee, on a turkey hunt at White Oak Plantation in Tuskegee, Alabama, recently. While there, Sefton shared with me his secrets for using a Woods Wise box call. Sefton took his first turkey in 1961. For years he refused to carry box calls with him hunting because he thought they were awkward. He also hated chalking them and trying to work with them wet. But ten years ago, while hunting with one of the Woods Wise pro staffers on a dirt road in Connecticut, he learned the value of a box call.

"I yelped on my diaphragm call and nothing answered," Sefton said. "Then I yelped on my slate call and other calls, and I still received no answer. The Woods Wise pro staffer I hunted with took out a box call and yelped on it. Four different turkeys

The benefits of using a box call are its harmonic notes, range of sound, and that turkeys are more likely to gobble at it than at any other call. (Credit: John E. Phillips, Night Hawk Pub.)

gobbled. From that day on, I've never been without a box call in the woods. I like a box call because it gives off harmonic notes, and a turkey will gobble at a box call more than at any other call. A box call has a lot of range, and you can get a turkey to answer you from even a quarter mile away when using one."

Sefton says to consider the following tips when using a box call:

- Don't pick the lid off the box. Remember that a box call, like any other friction call, only makes a sound in one direction. When you slide the paddle striker (lid) away from the box, it makes no sound. When you slide the paddle toward the box, it makes a sound. You want to maintain the proper angle with the striker by keeping it in contact with the call. If you pick the lid up, you'll change the angles and get unwanted squeaks and squawks from your box call.
- Use a very light grip, and keep a minimum amount of pressure on the lid. Use your fingers to guide the lid. How tight

you grip the lid will affect the sound of the call. Just barely move it.

- Hold the call by its bottom. When you touch it on the sides, you alter the sound of the call. You can get into a situation where you want to dampen the call by touching it on the side. But usually, you want to hold a call by its bottom so you can get the full effect of the call.
- Change the pitch of the call. Sometimes you can press your fingers on the side to dampen or change the pitch.
- Use cutts and cackles. These sounds are the best ones you can make on a box call. They're more realistic. If you're in the woods 100 yards away, and someone cutts and cackles on a box call, you'll swear it's a hen. And if there is a hen around when you cutt on a box call, she'll answer you. It's astounding how many times you'll get a hen to yelp at you after using the call.

More Tips for Using a Box Call

- Hold the call low to produce cutts and cackles. Hold your thumb on one side of the lid or on the back of the call, and use your thumb as a blocker so the lid can go only a certain distance. Then tap the lid or the striker on the other side, and tilt the call down, perpendicular to the ground, so that gravity will give you a series of clucks.
- Use no-chalk calls in the rain. The no-chalk coating on the call is impervious to moisture but is not waterproof. Although the call will be waterlogged and feel like it weighs 2 pounds, it'll still play because the gritty surface of the coating will allow it to maintain friction even when it's totally soaked.
- Don't warm your call in the oven. The heat will warp the box. Regardless of what box call you have, don't sand it. Box calls are built so that the curves and contours meet and

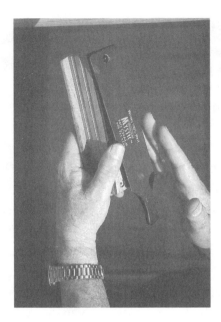

No-chalk calls will still play even if completely waterlogged. (Credit: John E. Phillips, Night Hawk Pub.)

match. These characteristics must remain the same so they get a consistent sound. Anytime you remove material from the wood on the box call, you change the concave and convex surfaces of the call, and it won't sound the same. I remember the old-timers who would sand their box calls before a turkey hunt. Don't sand your modern box calls. If a call needs sanding, then you probably need another box call. Calls today are tuned and set, so you don't want to change anything about them.

- Go with your individual tastes when buying a call. All box calls play the same. You have to determine what qualities you want in a call. You're the one who's going to have to play it. You have to have confidence in that box call when you set up to call a turkey. Before you buy any box call, you need to play the call and be satisfied that it sounds good to you.

- Use the best wood and avoid the bad wood when selecting calls. Everyone has different tastes. I want my box call to sound like a turkey. Walnut and poplar are two of my favorite woods to use in a call. Cedar sounds great, and any of the hardwoods are wonderful. Woods Wise has made good box calls out of sassafrass wood. I've also seen them made out of white oak, pecan and cherry. Any softwood or pine that isn't rigid makes a bad box call. You want a vibration in your call. You want that dense wood so the sound carries. Soft wood dampens the sound. If somebody makes a box call out of an orange box crate or pine, then it's not going to have the sound you need.

Tips for Caring for a Box Call:

- Secure the box call. Get some sort of elastic device to secure that box call while you walk. You don't want it yelping when you're walking down the road. You don't want to call anything you're not ready for, and you don't want to irritate your buddy. Any good, strong rubber band will work well. Get three different colors because you'll drop one and never find it again.

- Clean the box call. Box calls require very little maintenance. If your box call quits playing, you've gotten some oil or mayonnaise or something on it. If that happens to it, just take some dishwashing liquid or detergent and wash it, but don't dry it. It plays well while it's wet and will dry out on its own.

- Store your box calls. I always leave my box call in my hunting vest. If you have an antique or a special box call, don't take it hunting with you. You want to keep the box call you hunt with inside at room temperature and not in the barn where bugs may eat it. Box calls are low maintenance.

16

Patience is a (Turkey Hunting) Virtue

By Kathy Etling

When I crept into the pine grove well before dawn I already knew the spot was holding gobblers. I'd roosted the birds the evening before so I was sure that two, and maybe three, toms were now perched within 100 yards of my location. I waited, anticipating the hunt to come, savoring the possibilities. And when you're after the wily eastern wild turkey, missed possibilities are often the only thing left *to* savor at the end of the day.

When the first gobble pierced the woods, I gripped my shotgun tighter. Just maybe this would be the kind of hunt that all those guys on the videos seem to have; the kind where gobblers almost run you over in their eagerness to get to the calling. Usually, though, I work hard for my turkeys. And as the minutes passed, it looked like today would be no different. The turkeys

The author waited in suspense for nearly three hours.
(Credit: Bob Etling)

obstinately refused to come in, no matter how often I called, or which call I used. Finally, a hen moseyed past and headed towards the reluctant gobblers. As soon as the toms saw her, their reluctance disappeared. They flew off the roost and really started gobbling. Though they were now on the ground, it didn't help me a bit: From where I was sitting I still couldn't see them.

I waited in suspense for nearly three hours. The first hour was exciting. Gobbles rang out every couple of minutes, often in response to my calls, so I knew that *they* knew where I was. I hoped that once the boss gobbler tired of that particular hen, he'd be back for the one that wouldn't come in . . . me! But after three hours, I wasn't so sure. Oh, I'd hear a gobble every now and then, but never one that seemed really interested in me. No, they sounded more indifferent than anything else. Still, I remained where I was because I've been in the exact same predicament on many previous occasions, yet often had come home with a gobbler. So, I wasn't about to give up, not just yet in any event.

My patience paid off midway through the fourth hour. Patience? Perhaps, but maybe just sheer stubbornness. I hadn't heard a peep for close to twenty minutes and then I heard a single gobble, one that came from an entirely new direction than those I'd been listening to that morning. I eased my gun toward the sound just as a gobbler darted into view. When the bird moved behind a thick cedar tree, I shouldered my gun. I was waiting when he stepped out. Bead at the junction of neck and body, I squeezed the trigger and the gobbler tumbled to the ground. I jumped up to claim my prize and discovered a gobbler worth waiting for, one that weighed 23½ pounds, sported three beards—10, 9, and 6½ inches in length, plus 1¼-inch spurs.

You see, I didn't learn patience on my own. Back when I started hunting patience wasn't an option, it was a rule. My husband and I decided to try turkey hunting back in the mid-1960s, when the sport was still a novelty, even here in Missouri. We hadn't yet bought our own hunting ground, so we were fortunate to find a 400-acre farm where we could pay to hunt just an hour from our home. That farmer, whose name was John Dietzfelbinger, had very definite ideas about turkey hunting and safety. And I'm glad he did.

John would allot each hunter about 40 or so acres upon which to hunt. Each hunter had to remain on that parcel of land until he either killed a bird or decided to return to the house. Forty acres isn't much real estate, especially when you're turkey hunting. But I soon learned that it was *big enough*, providing I had enough patience.

I was soon lost in this newfangled sport with no one to teach me the basics. Even so, by faithfully remaining in a single spot where I made just three yelps on my box call every twenty minutes without fail, I called in a gobbler that very first year. It didn't matter much that he spotted me and ran away before I saw him. I'd learned a valuable lesson: Turkeys often will come sneaking in after gobbling just once or twice.

By the time I killed my first gobbler I could sit for hours in one spot. And once I'd bagged that first bird, I began killing toms regularly. Patience, I knew, worked. And yet when we finally bought our own land, I gave in to temptation and ran hog wild. It was wonderful having the freedom to chase birds anywhere. But when I did, my success rate plummeted. My calling hadn't changed, but the amount of patience I'd invested in my hunting sure had. I soon realized that my early successes were directly attributable to patience.

Most of us live life in the fast lane. One of the pitfalls of this lifestyle is expecting results . . . NOW! Many of today's hunting videos contribute to a mentality where anything less than instant gratification is not to be tolerated. They may make turkey hunting look like fun, but few tell the whole truth and nothing but the truth. Which is this: Unless you're an outstanding caller, hunting an area with little or no competition, turkey hunting can be anything but easy. The key to killing turkeys, no matter where you hunt, is patience. It's a key that a number of well-known turkey hunters use to consistently bag birds, experts like Georgia's Joe Drake and Missouri's Mark Drury, who used to hunt the farm next to John Dietzfelbinger's.

Of all the "pros" I've hunted with, Joe and Mark's tactics are closer to my own than anyone else's. "I learned the hard way," Joe confessed. "Moving too soon and bumping a bird coming in slowly or silently is the most common turkey hunting mistake, even among those who should know better. I've occasionally moved when I thought a bird wasn't coming in, then called from a new spot only to hear the gobbler answer from where I'd

Mark Drury and the author discuss hunting tactics.
(Credit: Bob Etling)

just left. Sitting and waiting can be frustrating. I know that. But possessing a high degree of patience is one of the most important skills or virtues you'll need to become a consistently successful turkey hunter, particularly if you're hunting areas where you regularly must compete with other hunters."

Joe's not only a top turkey hunter, he's also a world-class caller. Nevertheless, he rates patience higher than calling ability for consistent turkey hunting success. "When a bird gobbles several times in response to your call, he already knows where you are, so it's time to shut up," Joe explained. "Overcalling is a big problem today. Every hunter in the woods likes to hear himself call, so the birds quickly get call-shy. Hunters who head into the woods before the season begins for a few practice sessions aren't doing any of us a favor. It just makes gobblers warier, and that makes them more difficult to call in."

A double dose of patience is prescribed when you're after one of these call-shy birds, said Drake. "Turkey hunting has changed drastically in the last decade or so. Many more hunters are out in the woods, and all of them are calling—a lot! People like to say that today's turkeys don't gobble as much, and I believe that's true. They've been fooled before, either before or during the season, so why should they run in, gobbling their fool heads off? Better to proceed slowly and maybe save their necks.

"Some hunters go out, make a few loud calls from a ridgetop, and if a turkey doesn't run them down immediately they start looking for another bird. If hunting is tough—and turkey hunting gets tough, believe me—then patience is the only alternative. If a bird responds and I have the time I'll sit down, call once or twice, and then let him make up his mind whether to come in or not."

Joe's bagged many birds that other hunters felt were too cagey for killing. Like the bird that was holed up in a burn on some heavily-hunted public ground. "One hunter had been working this stubborn old gobbler ever since opening day," Joe recalled. "A couple of times I tried calling him, too, but didn't even get a response. One day I went by the burn again and did some cutting just to see if he'd answer. Hens cutt to demand a gobbler's attention, so cutting is a loud, long, insistent call. Anyway, it was almost noon so I was somewhat surprised to hear the gobbler answer me. I eased on into the burn, found a spot to set up, and yelped softly three times. The bird gobbled again from the same spot. I didn't call again for forty minutes, and he didn't gobble again either.

"Finally, I called. The tom gobbled directly behind my position. The bird had completely circled me and was so close I could actually hear him running toward me. I turned slowly so I could see him. It was sort of funny when I finally spotted him because with each step his foot would kick up a puff of soot from the burn. He slowed down, moved behind a tree, and when he stepped out I killed him."

Joe feels that patience has its place in calling, too. "Each time you call, you run the risk of stopping a gobbler and making him strut," he noted. "This is called 'hang-up time' since birds don't always gobble when strutting. Hunters who fail to hear constant gobbling may think the bird has lost interest. That's not always true. I've had some birds come in spitting and drumming, making that almost inaudible 'pfftt . . . boommm' sound that means they're puffed out and strutting. If you can hear that sound, the bird is already within shotgun range."

Waiting one and a half hours and even longer for a bird is not uncommon, according to Drake. He's waited as long as three hours waiting for a turkey to show. That's remarkable when you consider many top callers readily leave a gobbling bird if they don't feel he's "hot" enough. Instant success isn't always possible for ordinary hunters—hunters like me. I'm glad that Joe Drake and Mark Drury feel the same.

Mark's still a fairly young man and yet his turkey hunting experience would fill a couple of books. Growing up in prime Missouri turkey country, Mark already was an avid hunter by the time he was fourteen. He read everything he could on the subject until he became one of the top callers in the nation. Mark has won the Natural Voice World Calling Championship numerous times and yet he readily admits, "Sometimes the best call is no call at all.

"I do as little calling as possible," says this champion and founder of M.A.D. Calls, now a subsidiary of Outland Sports. "If I can get by with a couple of tree yelps, I'll leave it at that. The classic come-in, where a bird nearly runs you down, doesn't happen often. I'd guess only one out of every eight birds is that hot; otherwise, you really have to work for them."

Mark's known for persistence. His first longbeard taught him the value of patience. "I'd been playing 'cat and mouse' with this gobbler for a couple of hours," he explained. "I'd move too soon and he'd be just where I moved from. Finally, I sat down and waited him out. It took an hour before he finally appeared but when he did, he was mine."

Patience came in handy this past season as well. Mark and his brother Terry stayed after one gobbler for eight days before Terry finally killed the big 25½-pounder.

"I feel that being patient is as important as knowing the land you're hunting," Mark stated. "Those two factors together account for 75 percent of what it takes to succeed as a turkey hunter. Knowing turkeys' habits is worth another 15 percent. I really believe calling only counts for 5 or 10 percent. I know I can call, but I kill most of my turkeys by outmaneuvering, outsmarting, or outwaiting them."

Outwaiting a gobbler came in handy when Mark was hunting a Mississippi hardwood bottom many years ago. "I'd been after this really tough turkey," Mark explained. "On the third afternoon, I asked my friend, Randy Panek, if he'd like to come with me. We got into the area where I knew the gobbler had been and I yelped with my voice. He didn't answer, so I yelped again. This time the bird gobbled. When Randy and I got closer we could tell that the bird wasn't alone. He was with a whole group of turkeys on the other side of a cane thicket."

A big canebrake presents a formidable obstacle to a hunter. It can stop him flat in his tracks and that's exactly what this one did. Mark and Randy could hear the bird gobbling on the other side of the brake so they simply sat down where they were to call. "Our calling really got the flock fired up," Mark said. "Hens began calling and then the jakes began gobbling. Whenever the jakes gobbled, the boss would gobble, too. That went on for two hours before we wised up and shut up.

"When we got quiet, so did the turkeys. We were afraid they would leave so we began to call again. The turkeys got fired up all over again then everything began to die down. We could tell the flock was beginning to lose interest. We could also hear them starting to move away."

This particular Mississippi hardwood bottom was flat and open and studded with many huge trees. Cover was provided by several cane thickets, including the one near which they were hunting, but the two men realized that if they tried to move

The author's patience paid off with a first-rate gobbler.
(Credit: Bob Etling)

around the brake, the turkeys would spot them. The hunters' only option was to remain in the same spot where they'd spent the last three hours. As roost time approached, Mark realized that this was when the boss would be most vulnerable. He decided on a "jealousy" tactic and made a couple of jake yelps. They did the trick. The old bird responded immediately, and after hours of stalling, came charging toward the hunters' positions. In less than thirty seconds Mark and Randy saw the cane part and the gobbler appear. Randy killed that stubborn old bird when it was just 15 yards away.

If you finally want to get the upper hand on spring gobblers, try using a liberal dose of patience. Don't rely on gimmicks, or the "call of the year." Patience may be underutilized and underappreciated, but it's one turkey hunting tactic that will actually work!

Turkey-Taking Quiz

The Turkey-Hunting Game

By John Phillips

The game of turkey hunting is played in the turkey's backyard and on his terms. The strategies required to bag a tom turkey often may make war games look simple. The hunters who have amassed the most techniques, encountered the most turkeys and know what to do when the turkey doesn't do what he is supposed to do, will come home with bronze barons for dinner more often than other hunters. By taking this turkey-hunting quiz and learning what to do to bag turkeys, you can sharpen the skills that you will need in the woods when you play the game with the wisest wizards in the woods.

1. To take a turkey, you must first find a turkey. If you've done preliminary scouting and located a feeding area, a roosting area and a strut zone, yet failed to encounter the bird there,

where will you most likely find the turkey right after fly-down time?

a) the feeding area

b) the strutting zone

Answer: b) the strutting zone. Oftentimes, because of weather conditions or hunter pressure, the turkey may not feed or roost in the same place every day. However, more than likely, unless that tom has been disturbed, he will frequent a specific strut zone at the same time each day. Many hunters listen for turkeys to gobble in strut zones all during the day and set up timetables to try and intercept various turkeys at different strut zones throughout the day.

A typical strut-zone-hunting itinerary may read like this:

8:45 A.M.—Piney Woods Turkey strutting at the back of Bent Creek cow pasture.

9:45 A.M.—Canebreak Gobbler strutting on knoll of Elk Ridge.

10:57 A.M.—Beaver Pond Gobbler strutting between cow pasture and cornfield.

The hunter whose research tells him where and at what time these turkeys will consistently strut can put together a hunt plan so that he hunts three different strut-zone turkeys at three distinct times of the day.

2. The opening morning of turkey season has arrived. You have scouted for turkeys for two days prior to the opening of the season. Because of bad weather, you haven't heard a turkey gobble. You have put together no scouting plan that can tell you where the turkeys roost or feed. The only information you have to go on is that last year in this same woodlot you killed a gobbler.

What should you do?

a) go to the place where you killed a gobbler last year

b) keep attempting to make a turkey gobble

c) continue to scout, knowing that if you don't find a turkey, you will have more information to add into your hunt plan for the next day's hunting

d) go to areas where you think turkeys should be

Answer: a) go to the place where you killed a gobbler last year. Turkeys are creatures of habit, and they have a pecking order. When the dominant bird is harvested out of a flock, the next dominant bird will become the dominant gobbler. Usually the new dominant bird will gobble and strut in the same area where his predecessors gobbled and strutted, because the hens are already programed to come to this region during mating season to be bred. Therefore, the chances of killing a gobbler in the same place you killed a gobbler the year before are extremely good. Oftentimes you can take two gobblers the same year in the same place. I have known fellows who have bagged as many as four gobblers, where the season permits in the identical spot in one season.

3. You are hunting in a river-bottom swamp. You have located a turkey on the other side of a thigh-high slough. Which tactic will you use to take the bird?

a) try and call the turkey to the edge of the water and shoot him from the other side of the slough

b) run upstream or downstream and hope you find a crossing point

c) wade the slough and go to the turkey

d) attempt to call the turkey across the slough

Answer: c) wade the slough and go to the turkey. Although I have known hunters who have used all of the other tactics to move to turkeys, I believe that the best way to kill a turkey is to get close enough to call him and not put any natural obstructions like a creek or a slough between you and the turkey. If you've made the commitment to try

Two gobblers at the same time in the same place—a hunter's paradise! (Credit: John E. Phillips, Night Hawk Pub.)

and bag a turkey, then whatever is required to get into position to take a shot is part of the hunt.

Fooling Smart Turkeys

4. There are some smart turkeys that have been harassed by so many hunters that they will not come to calling. So a sportsman must decide whether he wants to call turkeys or kill turkeys. If the hunter has decided to take this bird, what is the best tactic to use?

    a) cluck three times and hush

    b) call a couple of times to determine which way a turkey is walking, circle the bird, get in front of him and don't call anymore, in hopes that he will walk in to where you are

    c) take a stand in the direction the turkey usually travels and wait on the bird to show up, but don't call at all

Answer: b) call a couple of times to determine which way a turkey is walking, and circle the bird, get in front of him and don't call anymore in hopes that he will walk in to where you are. Even if the gobbler answers going away from you, you should be able to determine a turkey's route of travel. With this information, you should have a pretty good guess of where to set up an ambush out in front of the gobbler.

5. When you are in an area that has a large number of hens, and the gobbler will not fly off of the limb or come to hen calling until he sees the female, how can you take the bird?
   a) use a turkey decoy if the procedure is legal in your state
   b) flush the gobbler, walk in the direction he flew off to and then attempt to call him back
   c) try and determine in which direction the hens normally feed after they meet the gobbler, don't do any calling, and take a stand on the hen's feeding route
   d) none of the above
   e) all of the above

   Answer: e) all of the above. Any of these tactics will work on toms that have a large supply of lady friends.

6. Some mornings turkeys don't gobble. However there are methods that can be used to make them gobble. What is the best tactic to use?
   a) use a crow call
   b) call loudly
   c) call like a bluejay
   d) begin to gobble

   Answer: a) use a crow call. The crow call is one of the most effective calls to use to get a turkey to shock gobble (gobble as a reaction to a stimulus rather than gobbling for mating purposes). There is just something about the high

The majestic tom in all his glory.
(Credit: John E. Phillips, Night Hawk Pub.)

pitch of a crow call that seems to make hush-mouthed gobblers talk.

7. In high-pressure areas where there are many hunters in the woods, when is the best time to bag a gobbler?

    a) in the mornings early before the other hunters get out in the woods

    b) late in the afternoon just before fly-up time

    c) in the middle of the day when no one else is hunting

    Answer: c) in the middle of the day when no one else is hunting. "I hunt in the middle of the day, because I've found that turkeys are less wary and easier to call in regions of high-hunting pressure," explains Harold Knight of Knight and Hale Game Calls in Cadiz, Kentucky. "Turkeys learn outdoorsmen's hunting patterns. After the season begins, most turkeys know that there will be fewer hunters in the woods from 10:30 A.M. until 2:30 P.M. than at any other time of the day. So that's when I hunt the hunter-shy gobblers.

    "Middle-of-the-day hunting is slow hunting because 75 percent of the time the turkey won't gobble before he comes in to where the hunter is waiting. I usually go to a place where two or three finger ridges come together into one hollow in an area where I know turkeys are supposed to be. Then I start calling and waiting. Many times I will wait an hour or two before I move. Usually, I never will hear the turkey until I see him. But there is a lot of good hunting in the middle of the day when other sportsmen are not in the woods."

Pulling a Gobbler Away from His Harem

8. One of the toughest turkeys to take in the spring is a gobbler that is traveling with a harem of hens. Calling a gobbler away from his harem is difficult. What can an outdoorsman do to call a gobbler away from his harem?

a) break up the flock, scatter the turkeys and call the gobler in to the hunter

b) try and slip in close enough to the flock to shoot the gobbler when the bird is standing away from the hens

c) attempt to call the hens to you hoping they will bring the gobbler with them

d) do some soft clucking, purring and yelping to sound like the most alluring hen the gobbler ever has heard

Answer: c) attempt to call the hens to you, hoping they will bring the gobbler with them. Hens have a pecking order just like gobblers do. Many times the boss hen—if she hears what she believes to be another boss hen trying to lure away her gobbler—will go to investigate her rival with the idea of running the rival off. In so doing, she will pull the flock to the hunter. The sportsman who can sit still and be calm enough to let hens walk by him may get a shot at the gobbler.

9. The worst thing that can happen when calling to a turkey is to have the gobbler circle you and come up behind you. You can hear the turkey strutting and drumming not 12 feet from you. What's the best tactic to use to take this turkey?

a) sit still and hope the turkey walks in front of you

b) roll over on your stomach and try and shoot the turkey

c) jump up and try and shoot the turkey

d) use your mouth caller and try and call the turkey to the front of you

Answer: a) sit still and hope the turkey walks in front of you. Rarely can a turkey hunter jump up and shoot a turkey before that turkey runs off. Even the hunter's rolling over gives the woods wizard too much notice of danger to catch the bird unprepared. If you try and call to the tom, the turkey will have to be out of his mind to figure he couldn't see a hen that he could hear that close by. So once again, patience is the key to getting a shot at this bird. Most of the time in this situation, only the most skilled hunter will be able to sit still long enough to bag his bird.

10. The best tactic for fall turkey hunting is scattering the flock and trying to call the turkeys back together again. What age bird does this tactic usually help take?

a) jakes (one-year-old gobblers)

b) longbeard gobblers

c) any type of gobblers

Answer: a) jakes (one-year-old gobblers). The jake is a young, inexperienced bird. His number one concern is being separated from the flock and finding mama. So after the flock is scattered, the jake is most often the gobbler that the hunter will have a chance to shoot in the fall.

11. Why do you use the owl hoot when hunting turkeys?

a) to call turkeys

b) to locate gobblers

c) to keep turkeys from coming too fast and too quickly

d) to locate hens.

Answer: b) to locate gobblers. Owl hooting will encourage turkeys to gobble. Many times when the turkey hunter is trying to move in closer on a gobbler to call to him, he needs to be able to keep up with that turkey's location without giving hen calls that will make the turkey come to him. So the turkey will gobble to the hunter's owl hooting and give away his location without actually coming to the hunter.

The No. 1 Turkey Call

12. In recent years, what did most turkey hunters believe was the number one call to get a turkey to come in quickly?

a) cackling

b) purring

c) cutting

d) soft yelping

Answer: c) cutting. Most hunters believe that the exciting clucks given in rapid succession known as cutting seem to arouse a gobbler quicker and cause him to come in to their blinds faster than any other type of calling. This is not to say that cutting is always the best call to use to draw a turkey in faster, but many experienced hunters have found that cutting is usually the most deadly call they utilize.

13. If you bag a turkey and you want to have him mounted, field dress the bird immediately.
    a) true
    b) false

    Answer: b) false. If you plan to have the gobbler mounted, get the whole bird refrigerated or frozen and to your taxidermist as soon as possible.

14. What's the easiest caller for beginning turkey hunters to use to call a turkey to within gun range?
    a) the slate call
    b) the diaphragm call
    c) the box call
    d) the push-button call

    Answer: d) the push-button call. All that is required to call a turkey with a push-button call is for the hunter to push a small wooden button back and forth. These box-type calls will give off an effective yelp and cluck and will make most any other sound that the wild turkey gives. It requires little or no skill in calling to work effectively.

15. Two-man turkey hunting is the most effective way to bag a gobbler.
    a) true
    b) false

    Answer: a) true. Team hunting often will allow sportsmen to take turkeys that they would be unable to bag using any other method. Two hunters on a tom often will produce

Here's a bird ready to be frozen or sent to the taxidermist.
(Credit: John E. Phillips, Night Hawk Pub.)

twice as much thinking, twice as much calling, and twice as many tactics to take one smart old bird.

16. To have an efficient shotgun for turkey hunting, you must have a barrel at least 30 inches long.

   a) true

   b) false

   Answer: b) false. Today's turkey hunter is opting for a shorter barrel more than ever before. The shorter barrel, if patterned with the right shells, can hold a tight pattern and requires less movement to aim than a longer barrel. The shorter-barrel shotgun is also easier to carry, especially when having to go through thick cover to get close to a turkey.

What to Do When the Turkey Comes Your Way

17. When you have a turkey coming toward you, what is the best thing to do?

   a) nothing

   b) call lightly to keep the bird interested

   c) call to him if he doesn't gobble in ten to fifteen minutes

   d) try and move closer to him

   Answer: a) nothing. Once the turkey knows where you are and is committed to come to you, there's no reason to call any more. The gobbler is doing what you wanted him to do. So, mount your gun, and prepare to take the bird.

18. When is the easiest time to kill a turkey?

   a) the first week of hunting season

   b) during the time that the hens are being bred

   c) the first week that the hens go on the nest

   Answer: c) the first week that the hens go on the nest. When the gobbler has been breeding, he continues to antic-ipate meeting his hens. When hens become scarce because they are on their nests, the old gobbler becomes even more anxious to find a willing hen. Therefore, he usually will move toward calling easier and quicker.

19. When you see turkeys in a field feeding, which is the easiest gobbler to take if there is more than one gobbler in the field?
    a) the turkey that gobbles back first when you call
    b) the gobbler with the most hens
    c) the tom with the fewest hens
    d) the gobbler with a few hens or no hens that struts when you call

    Answer: d) the gobbler with a few hens or no hens that struts when you call. Oftentimes, a subordinate gobbler will travel with a flock of turkeys. The boss gobbler usually will prevent the subdominant gobbler from breeding any of the hens in the dominant gobbler's harem. So when a subdominant gobbler hears a new hen yelp that is close to him, most of the time he will strut in hopes of attracting a hen that he can breed before a boss gobbler comes over to run him off.

20. What is the most critical factor in calling a turkey to where you want to take him?
    a) your ability to call
    b) your ability to be camouflaged well
    c) being in a place that a turkey naturally wants to go
    d) knowing where the turkey's roost tree is

    Answer: c) being in a place that a turkey naturally wants to go. If you have taken a stand along a route that a turkey naturally wants to travel, then the turkey will come by you without calling and will less likely see you if your camouflage is not just right. Many turkeys are bagged each season by hunters who call very little, if at all. They take their turkeys because they know where the toms want to go and are in the best place to meet those turkeys.

Tagging Late Season Toms

By Richard Combs

Richard Combs, a field editor for Bowhunting World *and* Ohio Sportsman *magazines, has written for many of the major outdoor publications. He is a dedicated outdoorsman with a passion for turkey hunting. His book,* Turkey Hunting Tactics of the Pros, *was published by The Lyons Press in 2001. He lives in Ohio.*

It's late in the turkey season, and you have yet to fill your tag. You're tired of getting up at 4 A.M. You've got blisters on your blisters and bug bites on your poison ivy. It's getting hotter every day, and the last few times you were out you heard a few distant gobbles on the roost, then nothing for the rest of the morning. And now your buddy called to tell you the bass are hitting at the local reservoir. I understand. You need some excuses to quit turkey hunting before season's end with your tag unfilled. I've got some excuses ready for you; I've used them myself. Here they are, free of charge:

"The toms are all henned up."

"The foliage is so thick this late in the season you couldn't see a tom if he walked up and tapped you on the shoulder."

"It's too hot to be out hunting."

"Too many turkey hunters out in the woods these days."

"By the second week of the season every tom out there runs the other way when he hears a hen yelp. It's a waste of time trying to call in a turkey that's been educated."

Before you pick up the phone to call your fishing buddy, though, let me counter those perfectly good excuses with a few reminders. First, let me remind you how much you looked forward to the season, and how short it is. Second, let me remind you that turkey hunting on the last day of the season can be better than on opening day. Finally, let me remind you how good you are going to feel as you hike across the meadow and through the woods with a big tom slung over your shoulder.

What you need is a game plan for late-season success. Start with an attitude adjustment and an equipment review. You know the birds are out there, Thousands of hunters will bag toms this year in the last week—on the last day, for that matter—of the season. You can be one of them if you put the time in and stay alert.

Okay, so it's hot in the woods and the bugs are out in force. Dress lighter, with a jacket or heavy shirt you can peel off and stuff in a day pack. Plan to soak your hat or a handkerchief in a nearby stream or pond—you'll be surprised how much that will cool you off. Take a cooler with soft drinks to leave in your vehicle. If you have to, take a brief break late in the morning for a cold drink. Don't plan to roam the hills prospecting for birds. Truth is, sitting tight in the shade in one or two spots can be just as effective. Turkeys move around. Let them come to you.

*Turkeys don't consult calendars. Late-season
hunting can be as hot as the weather.*
(Credit: Richard Combs)

As for the bugs, no problem. If turkeys had a sense of smell,
we'd never get a shot at one. They don't. Lather on the bug
dope and wear a headnet.

Next thing you need to do is develop a strategy. What has
prevented you from filling your tag up to this point? It could be
nothing more than a little bad luck. Even the most consistently

successful turkey hunters experience dry spells, when it seems they go for many days without bagging a tom.

Many frustrated beginning turkey hunters suspect their calling is not up to snuff. Calling well enough to fool a turkey is not difficult, but confidence in calling is essential. The cadence, or rhythm, of the calling is more important than perfect tone. Calling is a subject in itself, but if you are concerned about this, I'd suggest you play a cassette tape of turkey calls in your car on your way to hunt. While practice at other times is important, by listening to hen yelps immediately before you hunt, the proper cadence will be fresh in your mind.

Chances are, though, that your calling is not the problem. Could be the toms really are henned up. If you hear some gobbling early on the roost, then none or very little after fly down time, there is a very good chance the toms are with hens. If toms seem to move in your direction, but repeatedly fade away, listen carefully for hen yelps in the background, a sure sign hens are with the gobbler.

Calling in a flock of hens is difficult, but if you can do it the toms will usually follow. Some experts suggest challenging the boss hen with aggressive yelping and cutting. I've rarely been able to make that work, and when I have brought hens in that way the gobbler is usually lagging behind, and the large number of alert hens pecking around me has made it impossible to get in position for a shot at the gobbler.

What has occasionally worked for me is a trick I picked up many years ago from two-time world champion turkey caller Larry Norton, who guides professionally at Alabama's Bent Creek Lodge.

"More often than not, explains Larry, "if you challenge the hens, they'll just move away from you and take the gobbler with them."

Instead, Larry tries to slip close enough to the birds that he can hear quiet, contented calls. Understand that he is not talking about stalking to within shotgun range of the birds, which is not only very difficult to do, but is unsafe as well. On a calm day, though, turkeys can hear quiet calls from 70 or 80 yards at least. In some cases, hens that would run from aggressive calling will move in the direction of quiet calls, possibly thinking they're hearing a member of their own flock.

Outdoor writer and long-time Ohio turkey chaser Tom Cross often uses a tactic similar to Norton's, though it is the gobbler and not the hen's attention he wants to get.

"A gobbler doesn't want to get out of sight of his hens," Tom once explained to me. "But if you figure out which way the turkeys are moving, get ahead of them and set up in a spot where all the gobbler has to do is peek over a bank or take a few steps around a bend to see what he thinks is a hen calling, he'll usually do it."

Tom takes advantage of hills, and of the thick foliage in the late season, to get close enough to gobblers to tease them into taking a peek at him.

Other turkey hunters have made the same discovery, and some refer to it as getting inside a gobbler's comfort zone. While there is some disagreement about exactly how close that is, most hunters agree that within a certain distance, a gobbler is much more likely to respond to calls. Hunters should understand, though, that is never the first strategy to try, but should be saved for a last-ditch effort, since moving in close risks spooking the bird and bringing the duel to a rapid and unsatisfactory conclusion. Safety is as always paramount, and hunters must use good judgment about how close is "close." There will be other days and other duels, and no gobbler is worth risking one's safety for.

Keep in mind, too, when every gobbler seems to have hens, that this will change, and when it does the change can be abrupt. Don't assume the toms are with hens today because they were yesterday.

Regardless of what the turkeys are doing or why they're doing it, it only makes sense in the late season to take advantage of the greenery to move in a little closer to them. If you set up at 150 or 200 yards from a roosting tom in the early season, you should be able to close that distance to 100 yards, possibly a little less, in the late season. As the woods green up and the foliage grows thicker, gobblers will sound farther away, and it's important to allow for that.

Another advantage of late season hunting, assuming you've been after them since opening day, is that by late in the season you've probably been able to pattern some birds. If turkeys were totally predictable they wouldn't survive, but they do have their favorite roosting areas, their favorite feeding and strutting areas, favorite places to loaf in the shade when the sun gets high, and so forth. They also have their favorite travel lanes between these areas. And though turkeys are not often associated with funnels as deer are, the fact is that turkeys can be funneled by fences, ravines, streams and ridgetops in their travels just as can deer. And they are even more likely than deer to take advantage of trails and timber haul roads.

It can be an effective tactic, if birds are not being vocal or responding readily to calls, to set up an ambush in one of these areas. I generally like to have several such areas as backups whenever I turkey hunt. I spend the first hour or so trying to locate a bird on the roost. After that, I respond to any gobbling I hear. However, if I spend an hour or so of hearing not a single gobble, I'll put decoys out in a meadow, or sit along a ridgetop trail or a haul road that experience has told me the local turkeys use heavily. Most of the turkeys I have taken in these areas have come in to my calling, but as any experienced turkey hunter will tell you, it's much easier to call in a tom that was already headed in your direction.

It's very important, when hunting the call-shy gobblers of the late season, to stay alert for toms sneaking in to your calls. Some turkey hunters bag only the gobblers that come in strutting and gobbling. Those hunters are not bagging nearly as many gobblers as they could. More toms will sneak in than will strut in announcing their presence, and this is particularly true in the late season. It's imperative that you get comfortable enough in your setup to remain absolutely still. Scan the surroundings with your eyes, looking for the slightest movement or the white head of a gobbler. If you must turn your head, do it very slowly. Keep you gun in a shooting position across your knees at all times. If you don't, a bird will slip in on you and you'll watch in frustration as he wanders off without giving you a shot, or you'll try the quick draw routine and most likely shoot air.

While it is true that gobblers become warier, more call-shy and less inclined to gobble as the season progresses, it is not true, as some hunters contend, that the birds leave areas of heavy hunting pressure. Radio telemetry studies have demonstrated on numerous occasions that turkeys that are spooked will run or fly no more than a few hundred yards. If badly spooked, they may sit in a tree for an hour. In most cases they return to normal behavior within ten or twenty minutes. And they don't leave the area.

Hunters can in some cases greatly influence the extent to which turkeys become harder to hunt as the season progresses. Those fortunate enough to own, lease, or have exclusive access to hunting properties can avoid educating birds by employing less aggressive hunting methods, at least early in the season. Especially on the relatively smaller tracts of land common in the

East and Midwest, hunters can select one or two good strut zones to watch, putting out a few decoys and calling birds in instead of chasing them through the woods to play cat and mouse games. It requires more patience and discipline than "run and gun" tactics, but in the long run, assuming the hunter has scouted well and knows the area, it is at least equally effective.

More and more hunters are using blinds in the turkey woods, and this goes hand in hand with less aggressive hunting

Keep gobblers responding to calls all season long by setting up blinds near field edges or other strut zones. (Credit: Richard Combs)

styles. Small, portable blinds can be quickly erected or taken down. In much the same way deer hunters access tree stands, turkey hunters can hunt one or two spots, accessing these spots and traveling between them along routes less likely to disturb turkeys from roosts, strut zones, or travel corridors. The result can be turkeys that gobble more throughout the season, and are generally less wary and call shy. If a tag remains unfilled late in the season, hunters can then resort to more aggressive tactics.

For instance, some hunters resort to fall hunting tactics when all else fails. They cover ground until they bump birds off logging roads, trails, or meadows, then try to call the birds back together. Another last-ditch tactic: Roost birds, then get between a gobbler and his hens and flush them off the roost, either in the evening or morning. Sometimes the hens will roost far enough from the gobbler that a hunter can flush the hens without flushing the gobbler. If the gobbler flushes, that is not necessarily a problem unless he moves off in the same direction as the hens—which shouldn't happen assuming the hunter has succeeded in getting between them. The gobbler will be eager to get back to the hens, and will often be very susceptible to calling, especially if flushed off the roost the evening before. It's important, when using this tactic, to stay between the gobbler and hens, and keep the hens away from the gobbler if at all possible. If they get to him before he's in shooting range, the game is over.

If turkey hunting were easy, everyone could do it. It can be tough. As with most endeavors, though, the harder you have to work at it, the more satisfaction you feel upon achieving success. Put in the time and do the work, and you can be one of the thousands of turkey hunters carrying a late season gobbler out of the spring turkey woods.

Fall Turkey Tactics

By John McDaniel

John McDaniel is a professor of anthropology at Washington and Lee University. He authored The Lyons Press book, The American Wild Turkey, *which was published in 2001. He divides his time between Montana and Virginia.*

The popularity of spring turkey hunting has increased dramatically in recent years. Most of us who hunt turkeys enjoy the spring season tremendously. However, I am afraid that the interest directed to spring hunting has resulted in hunters overlooking the opportunities available in the fall.

For the individual who wants to enjoy an introduction to turkey hunting, the fall season provides significant advantages over a spring hunt. Of primary importance is that the fall hunt offers an opportunity to harvest young birds. For the beginner or the relatively inexperienced hunter, the young bird affords a predictability that is not available with mature spring gobblers.

The first step—finding a flock—is the most difficult. A key that will increase your odds is to plan your available hunting time so that you hunt as many consecutive days as possible. Assuming that you are in good turkey country, the chances of finding a flock are increased immeasurably if you can dedicate a number of consecutive days to the search. The consecutive days allow you to eliminate certain areas the birds are not using. The "scratching" sign the birds leave behind in their search for food will provide evidence of the flock several days after they have worked the area. Consecutive days allow you to eliminate broad areas as you hunt. In contrast, if you decide to hunt five separate days during the season, the decision not to investigate an area that was not being used on your previous hunt becomes a dangerous strategy. The glade that was not used two weeks ago may be where the turkeys are now! Another advantage of consecutive days is that they allow the hunter to return to a spot at which he scattered birds the day before. Despite much literature to the contrary, even birds scattered before noon will often wait until the next day to regroup.

A second key factor contributing to the ease with which a hunter can find fall turkeys is for him to cooperate with a friend. To find flocks of turkeys consistently, one must cover many acres. Two men can cover twice as much area. A friend of mine and I hunt in different areas on the first day. If one of us encounters birds or fresh sign, the information is communicated in the evening, and the next day the two of us will cooperate in an intensive hunt. It is my conviction that this technique more than doubles our chances of encountering fall birds. The lone hunter, frustrated by failure in finding a flock, will often become discouraged. The hunter who knows his friend is investing a similar effort is more likely to work hard in his own zone of responsibility.

My own partner and I have become great believers in the advantages conferred by the use of a dog to find fall turkeys.

Hunting with a dog has certain advantages during fall turkey hunting. (Credit: John McDaniel)

The dog does not have to be a supremely trained turkey dog; however, he must respond well to the hunter and resist the temptation to chase game other than turkeys. My grouse dogs, Brittany spaniels, work very well as turkey finders. The enjoyment they derive from scattering a flock of turkeys in no way has detracted from their grouse performances. On several occasions, it has been during successful grouse hunts that the dogs have encountered flocks of turkeys. The dogs will not only increase the number of flocks found, but they also scatter the birds much more effectively than the hunter can. The key again is not to *scare* a flock but to *scatter* it. If the birds fly off together, they will not need to get back together, and the opportunity to call the separated birds is lost. A dog all but assures the effective dispersion of any flock you encounter. Since my dogs are not trained to lie in the blind without moving after the birds have been scattered, I take them back to the car before returning to call the turkeys. In most instances, my return takes place early the next morning; however, if I do scatter birds in the morning, I usually can be back at the blind within an hour.

Fall turkeys are much easier to find when snow is on the ground. If you are lucky enough to be able to hunt at short notice, there is no better situation to take advantage of then snow. Last year, on three occasions we used snow to find turkeys. The fact that turkeys must feed during the day means that the speed with which a flock travels is not too great. The persistent hunter will usually find a flock within an hour or two of taking up a fresh trail. In many instances, when the flock is encountered they will flush within shotgun range. The ability to get relatively close is, of course, dependent on the nature of the terrain and cover and the size and composition of the flock. A fresh snow also provides a tremendous advantage for the hunter with respect to recovering crippled birds.

Once the birds have been found and scattered, the hunter faces the challenge of calling the birds back to him. A first step to success at this stage of the hunt is to build an effective blind. The primary criterion which will determine the success of the blind is its location. If you use a good call from the correct position, your changes of killing a fall turkey are high. If you use an excellent call from a poor position, your chances are poor. The blind should be near the spot from which the birds flushed. It is often true that if it is slightly uphill it will work perfectly, but I have made the error of placing a blind too far above the flushing sport only to watch the birds regroup below me.

I believe in a well-constructed and comfortable blind. I have been much more successful shooting from a well-constructed blind than from sitting up against a tree. A good blind does not obviate the need for some personal camouflage, but it makes total camouflage unnecessary.

A well-constructed blind will afford good concealment; however, the hunter must attempt to keep all movements within the

*Be sure the major cross supports on your blind can hold
the weight of a gun.* (Credit: John McDaniel)

blind to a minimum. One of the disadvantages of a blind is that
it convinces the inexperienced hunter that he can move at will
within it. Nothing could be less true. The turkey is capable of locating hunter movement within even well-constructed blinds.
Gun movement is particularly important. In most cases, the
hunter can prepare for the arrival of the turkey. Most turkeys can
be heard walking or calling as they approach. The gun should be
mounted and then the barrel rested over a suitably sturdy part of
the blind that faces the direction from which the turkey is approaching. I specifically check the major cross supports on my

blinds to be assured they can hold the weight of a gun. When the turkey steps into view, all that is necessary is a slight adjustment in the direction of the barrels. This final adjustment should be made when the bird is either behind cover or looking away from the blind. Attempts to pull the gun up quickly are usually futile.

If you have selected a good location for your blind, calling a young wild turkey in the fall is not too difficult. The basic calls are the whistling kee-kee run and the high-pitched yelp of the young hen. It will bring young turkeys on the run. The young hen will usually be much easier to call than the young gobbler. In many cases hens will come on the run to the first few hen yelps you make. Do not be bashful about making enough calls. A young turkey expects another lost bird to be eager to regroup.

The best type of call for the fall turkey hunter is one of the diaphragm-type calls readily available on today's market. If you are ready to invest the effort that is required of a turkey hunter, I am sure you have the degree of patience necessary to learn to use the diaphragm call. This call is best because it provides the best imitation of the calls used by turkeys, particularly young turkeys. The kee-kee is indispensable to the fall hunter, and this call cannot be made with the box. One can learn to use a diaphragm call with the instructions provided with it; however, the time required to master the call will be reduced significantly if you can locate an individual who can teach you. In addition, there are now many fine records and tapes available that the hunter can imitate as he practices. The best way to conduct such practice is to record your own calls on a small cassette tape recorder and then compare them to those on the records. Once you have learned the basic techniques, it is essential that you continue practicing with the call. One great advantage of the diaphragm is that you can practice in so many situations; for example, as you drive to work or watch a poor TV show.

After mastering the basic calls, the hunter must still learn when to call. If I have scattered a flock of young turkeys in the afternoon, I will build a blind at the spot from which they flushed and wait for evening. I will be surprised, but ready, if the flock tries to regroup before dark. If they do not, I will use my compass to make sure I am capable of returning to the precise spot before light the next morning. In the afternoon, I will only call in response to birds calling.

The next morning, I will be in the blind before light. Sometimes the birds will begin to call shortly after dawn; on other occasions there will be no calls for the first fifteen minutes of light. In the latter cases, I will make several kee-kee calls. In most cases I will get a response to these calls. Be sure to wait for the answer to your first calls, as often it will come after several minutes pass. Those several minutes can seem long indeed. When the young bird does respond, I try to imitate the call the bird makes; usually it will be a clean, whistling kee-kee whistle or the high-pitched yelp of a young hen. At this juncture you should be ready for rapid development. On one occasion, I responded to a young hen yelp with a couple of high-pitched yelps, and, before I could warn the hunter I had with me, two young hens sprinted to within 5 yards of the blind. Once a bird is on its way and calling with some frequency I will call back about once for every three calls the bird makes. When the bird is within 75 yards it will often cease its yelping and begin to cluck. I will imitate these clucks as the bird closes the final distance. By this time you usually will be able to hear the bird walking toward you. Once the bird is this close I quit my calling, raise my gun, and wait. I try to shoot my birds at about a 25-yard range. You may read about 60-yard turkey guns, but no experienced turkey hunter will take a shot at a bird coming to his call at over 45 yards. On the other hand, if you let a bird come too close, you have precious little pattern to operate with. Twenty-five yards is a nice range. Hold for the head and neck, and concentrate. Just because you are shooting at a sitting bird doesn't allow you to be careless. A good shot, and good friend, once missed a gobbler at a measured 30 yards because he was shooting downhill and failed to place his head down on the comb on his stock.

Before you invest in a specific gun for your fall turkey hunting, I suggest you talk to a few hunters with experience. I have killed turkeys with five different types of guns, and it is my conviction that for most of the opportunities presented in turkey hunting a shotgun is the best choice. I suggest you use the largest shotgun you can shoot and carry effectively. The over/under rifle-shotgun combinations that look great in sporting-goods stores do not provide the firepower you will need in many situations. I can think of three cases in which I flushed flocks while carrying an over/under combo. In all three cases I missed a first, quick shot with the shotgun and then watched with frustration as birds flushed back over me in easy range. I have also used drillings—the European guns that offer two shotgun barrels over a rifle barrel. Again, this theoretically seemed to be the perfect choice; pragmatically, it has numerous disadvantages. Of primary importance is its complexity. The barrel selector is on the tang, where a safety should be. Also, the hair trigger for the rifle barrel and the strange position of the safety make it a difficult gun to learn to shoot quickly.

It may be a function of the areas I hunt in, but my records show that for every good rifle shot I get at turkeys, I will have ten chances that could be handled better by a shotgun. If you have a long-range shotgun that is suitable for long-range waterfowl hunting, you have a fine turkey gun. If you are buying a gun exclusively for turkey hunting, I suggest you buy either a 10-gauge or a 3-inch Magnum 12-gauge with a full-choke barrel that is capable of providing at least two quick shots.

The most critical factor relevant to any gun is your ability to use it effectively. If you have a 2¾-inch 12-gauge with a full-choke barrel that you shoot well and a new 10-gauge that you shoot poorly, the obvious choice is the 12. However, if you are equally capable with both guns, the more potent is the best.

There are two major threats to the successful implementation of the fall strategy discussed above. First, the flock you scatter may not consist of young turkeys but rather old gobblers. In this case the birds will not respond to the same calls. In addition, the old birds are far more difficult to call even if you can imitate their coarse yelps and deep clucks. The inexperienced hunter should be suspicious about the composition of flocks that are small. A flock of three to six big birds is probably composed of old gobblers. A search for tracks and sign in the area the birds flushed from can help determine the sex of the birds.

Gobbler tracks are usually over 4¼ inches long from tip of middle toe to heel. Gobblers and hens of the year and adult hens will measure under this length. Finally, the droppings of the birds can be used to determine sex. Most gobbler droppings are characterized by a "hook" at one end—an element that is lacking from those of the hen. The beard is the most obvious sex characteristic to use in identifying birds as they run or flush in front on you. One should be aware that this feature is often difficult to see in flight.

If you do scatter a flock of old gobblers, I suggest you follow the steps outlined above with two critical exceptions. First, you must make calls that old gobblers expect their friends to make. These calls will be deep yelps and coarse clucks. Perhaps the most critical factor is that old gobblers call infrequently and take longer to regroup. Mature gobblers are very tough to fool.

If the flock is large, it is highly probable that it is composed of hens and their young. These flocks will vary in size but most flocks I encounter average about ten to twelve birds.

When a flock of hens and young birds is scattered, a major threat to the strategy we have discussed is the old hen herself. As you call, you may find you are competing, unsuccessfully, with the hen in an attempt to attract the birds back. The old hen will establish a regrouping spot near the point at which the flock was dispersed and begin to yelp incessantly as she calls her brood. Do not try to compete with the hen; rather, flush the hen and chase her from the area. If you fail to chase the hen off, all the young birds will go to her.

Do not give up if you call a young bird up and miss it. Young turkeys will often come to a blind after another bird has been shot at. Just last season there were two occasions when I called several birds up from the same flush. On one occasion, a third bird, a young hen, was called after two birds had come and been shot at and missed. I do not believe the sound of a gun causes great panic to the turkey. The human voice will not be tolerated, but the gun must sound like crashing trees or thunder to the bird and is not inherently frightening. I have noticed that birds that come after a shot has been missed are often silent. The third bird that came to our blind on that one incredible morning did not make a sound. Listen intently for the sounds of movement. One soon learns how important hearing is for the identification of turkeys.

The popularity of the spring season is not unjustified. On the contrary, all of us who love turkeys enjoy the thrills of the spring hunt; however, do not relegate your hunting of turkeys to the spring alone. The turkey provides great sport in the fall as well. The thrill of a new snow and the knowledge that you will probably find the flock somewhere on the mountain the next day is intoxicating. In addition, the roosting of a gobbler in the spring is not nearly as "sure" as is busting a flock late in the afternoon in the fall. Anticipation consists of relaxing in a hot bath after a great day in cold, November woods when you have found turkeys and scattered them. The next day you should have turkeys close.

Don't relegate the king of the uplands to the spring. Try him on the all-day hunts of the fall.

Afternoon on
Chinquapin Hill

By Lovett Williams

Former Chief of the Bureau of Wildlife Research in Florida, Lovett Williams has been a private wildlife management consultant, corresponding editor of Turkey & Turkey Hunting *magazine, author of books about wild turkey biology and hunting, and owner of Real Turkeys audiocassettes and turkey hunting products. Lovett has degrees in zoology, wildlife management, and a Ph.D. in wildlife ecology.*

When I started hunting turkeys in the 1950s, there was no spring gobbler hunting and calling turkeys was a little known art in northern Florida where I lived and hunted. My turkey hunting strategy came straight from squirrel hunting—I would sit where I found field sign and hope to bushwhack a turkey when one came that way again. I learned a lot about reading sign, gained much respect for the stealth and pure magic of turkeys, and killed a few unlucky turkeys that way, but mostly I came out of the woods empty-handed at dark wondering where the turkeys had been that day. Experiences of one November afternoon turned my fall turkey hunting strategy around and put me in quest of learning the fall vocabulary of the wild turkey.

I was moving slowly through the woods all day looking for turkey sign. Along the edge of an oak grove overlooking the swamp I came across enough fresh turkey sign to make a nine-teen-year-old dizzy. Turkeys had been there that morning scratching under the chinquapin trees. I pulled down a limb, broke off a small cluster of chinquapins, and sat down among the turkey scratchings. I had been in the woods since before day-light. I sat down in the leaves and soon laid back and fell asleep.

The next sound I heard was the ticking of tiny rain drops in the leaves near my ears. Then there were louder stirrings with a rhythm I recognized. I was surrounded by a flock of turkeys scratching for any chinquapins they had missed this morning. As I slowly reached for the Model 12 pump beside me, two loud putts confirmed that turkeys were there and that my movement has not gone unnoticed. As I bolted upright, turkeys were moving in all directions like in fast forward while I fumbled with my safety in slow motion. I managed to get off three shots—one while seated, one on my knees, and one as I was falling over sideways from the recoil of the second shot. For a few minutes I just stared out over the swamp where the turkeys had disappeared. I picked up my cap and the three empty shells beside my dry body imprint in the crushed leaves and spent a few minutes looking at the fresh turkey scratching less than 50 feet away.

By the time I got to the hard road, the rain was pelting down hard but it didn't drown out the sounds of wingbeats that still rang in my ears.

Not long after that a friend gave me a copy of *The American Wild Turkey* by Henry Davis—the only turkey book I had seen or heard of. I read it in lieu of a weekend assignment in World History 102, or was it Chemistry?

Anyway, Davis said the hardest part of fall turkey hunting was scattering the turkeys, but that when you do, it's not so hard to call them back. If he was right, I could think of at least six missed opportunities already that season. That is, *if* he was right. I would soon find that out.

Scattering is the Key

It didn't take long to confirm to my satisfaction that scattering and calling is indeed the essence of fall turkey hunting. In fact, I think Davis understated the need to get a good scatter. After that fall hunting season, seeing a flock flying away in all directions was a welcome beginning, not the end, of an exciting and usually successful fall turkey hunt. And that is when I began to keep notes and make a study of fall turkey hunting and especially the turkey's calls.

Scattering from the roost is the best way. To find roosting places, I listen for wingbeats at sundown and study field sign. Or somebody may tell me where a known roost is. As I move into a roosting flock, I force the turkeys in different directions to do a good job of scattering. Turkeys flushed from the roost usually fly only about 150–250 yards and land in trees. I pay close attention to the direction they go so I can follow up for further scattering.

When scattered from the evening roost, turkeys get over their fright during the night and assemble quickly the next morning. So it's a good practice to scatter them again in the morning even if you flushed them the evening before.

One way to find a fall turkey flock that's not on the roost is to move quietly and listen for scratching during prime feeding

*A roosted turkey has no option but to fly when frightened
and, when flushed, will usually land in another tree
150–250 yards away.* (Lovett E. Williams)

hours. When only a few turkeys are scratching, you will hear
the characteristic rhythm of four scratches—scratch . . . [pause]
. . . scratch–scratch . . . [pause] . . . scratch; then a repeat of the
four-scratch rhythm. Under optimum conditions, you can hear
a flock scratching from 200 yards away. If you hear turkeys
scratching late in the day, and can ascertain their direction of
travel, and follow them to their roost.

Scattering a flock on the ground can be difficult. Every flock
has been scattered before and the birds know that regrouping is

easier when they all move in the same direction. I do everything possible to scatter some of the turkeys in opposite directions, or they will assemble with little yelping and offer no hunting opportunity. If you have to flush turkeys on the ground, get as close as possible and startle the flock.

Fall Calling

Scattered young turkeys are desperate for company and are very vocal. They are much fun to call because they use a wider vocabulary than spring gobblers do. Fall calling is the way to really talk to the turkeys and not just at them. I have found a few reliable rules for fall turkey calling.

Set up within shotgun range of the place the family flock was flushed. The first calling heard will usually be a *kee-kee* less than one hour after a morning scatter. I usually call back with a kee-kee as soon as I hear a turkey calling. If nothing is heard for an hour after the flush, I stimulate calling by giving a few kee-kees myself. It is a rare day that I won't get an answer soon after beginning to call.

Late season turkeys may respond to your first calls by giving the *hush call* or the *chattering call*, both of which mean you have called too soon after the flush. When you recognize one of these weird precautionary calls, you can take satisfaction that you have already fooled a turkey—it thinks it is warning an anxious flock mate. When it is time for the young turkeys to start calling, you will hear no further warning calls.

As they assemble, young fall turkeys use the *kee-kee-run* more than any other call. When a lost turkey is called close but is unable to see the responding turkey (or you), it may stop and sound the *plain cluck* as a request for the other turkey to approach. You should stay put to make him show himself. And don't call again for awhile—he knows where you are from hearing you call and he might spot you if you move. If that happens, you'll hear an *alarm putt* and no more calling from that turkey for an hour or more. But the hunt will still be on for the others that haven't been spooked. Other calls you may hear on a fall hunt are *cutting* by a turkey searching for the flock and *cackling* at flying down time.

Sooner or later a brood hen will sound off with the *brood assembly yelp* which will probably be one of the last calls you will hear that morning. The usual example is loud and long yelping with a commanding air about it. I have no proof that such a call is made only by the brood hen, but I think so because when you hear it, the young turkeys stop calling and head toward its source.

Even after the brood hen calls, there are usually a few lost turkeys too far away to hear the assembly command if you scattered them well. Have lunch and a nap and hunt the same place that same afternoon. If you had a good scatter, your chances are as good in midafternoon as they were in the morning.

If you scatter a flock of all jakes, you won't have to worry about the old hen's assembly yelp. The tactics used on family flocks apply. But if you scatter a flock of adult turkeys, there will be less calling and assembly may take several hours or even days. The calls you hear will be single and double yelps, lost yelping, and clucking. No kee-kees or kee-kee-runs and no assembly yelping of the brood hen. Sometimes you hear no calling at all as the adults assemble as if by magic. Adults are a challenge and that includes old hens that are not associating with broods. When up against adults, use lost yelping and respond with the calls you hear the turkeys using. And be very still and very patient.

I hunted the same woods near on Chinquapin Hill often and always saw tracks and other sign. But I never again saw as many scratchings or as many chinquapins on the trees as I did that overcast afternoon in November. When I passed that way, I always found the exact spot I took that nap and shook my head to think about the afternoon I left the woods just before the hunt began.

The "C" in World History 102 that semester because I read *The American Wild Turkey* instead of the history book didn't help my grade point average but I wouldn't have had it any other way.

THE CALLS FOR FALL TURKEY HUNTING

Name of call	Comment/meaning
Kee-kee	The basic call of lost young turkeys/"I'm lost"
Kee-kee-run	Assembly call of lost young turkeys/"I'm lost too"
Tree yelp	Wake-up call on roost/"Good morning, I'm still here"
Cackle	Occasionally sounded by a flying turkey
Lost yelp	Assembly call of adults/"I'm lost, where are you?"
Single & double yelp	Lost call of cautious turkeys/"Let's get together"
Cutting	Search call of turkey or flock/"Where are y'all?"
Plain cluck	By a called-up turkey/"Here I am, show yourself"
Hush call	A precautionary call/"Shut up, stupid"
Chattering call	A precautionary call/"Watch out, danger is near"
Assembly call of hen	"Ya'll stop your calling and come here right now"
Alarm putt	"I see you, sneaky hunter—Bye"

Twenty Mistakes Turkey Hunters Make

By Gerald Almy

S uccessfully harvesting a spring gobbler is one of the most difficult challenges in hunting. It's not uncommon to hear of some sportsmen spending years searching for that elusive first bird. Others may strike pay dirt early, then hit a dry spell for several seasons. If you're facing one of these situations, it's time to analyze your past hunts and tactics and see if you can pinpoint some mistakes that you can eliminate that might have cost you the chance to bag a majestic gobbler.

I can speak as a pro on this subject, because over the years I have probably made every mistake in the book.

Here are twenty of the most common mistakes turkey hunters make and tips on how to avoid them.

Not Scouting Enough

This is one you can remedy now, before the season opens. It's vital to put in enough time before the season starts in your hunting area to know where the birds are, the lay of the terrain, good calling locations and where your best fall-back spots will be if someone else is parked where you first hoped to go. That last factor is one of the most vital reasons to preseason scout.

The woods are getting more and more crowded with turkey hunters. You need several birds located before the season arrives, so if someone is in your first choice of areas, you can quickly head to another spot nearby. Also, some toms may simply not gobble one day in a certain area. If you have other places you feel confident in from scouting, you can head to them quickly and perhaps find a more vocal bird.

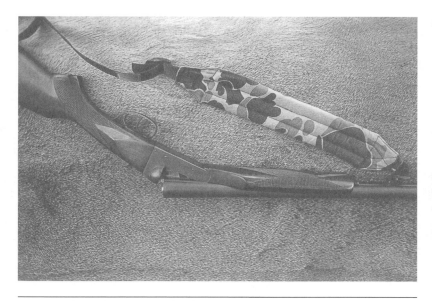

Use the right gun and loads, and don't forget to load the gun!
(Credit: Gerald A. Almy)

Not Loading Your Gun

Seem impossible? Not so. I've heard of many hunters who have made this mistake. It's especially likely to happen if you get in a hurry. Allow yourself plenty of time to eat, collect your gear, drive to the hunting area, calmly check your gear for vital items, and load up. If it's dark or you have a long, rough hike in to the hunting spot, you can wait and stuff shells in when you get there. But be sure you have a mental checklist system worked out so you don't forget this crucial step. It's a sickening feeling to squeeze the trigger carefully on a bird you've worked so hard to lure into clean killing range and hear a tiny snap instead of a loud explosion.

Driving Too Close to the Hunting Spot

If the first glimmer of predawn is approaching as you are pulling up to the hunting area, there's a natural tendency to drive a bit closer so you can get to the birds more quickly. Avoid it. It's better to be a bit late than to drive up so close that birds can hear the truck engine and doors opening and shutting.

Even if a tom doesn't spook and fly away with wildly flapping wings, he's likely going to be suspicious and reluctant to come in to your calls if he's heard human voices or vehicles nearby. Park at least a quarter mile away from where you plan to hunt. In some cases half a mile is better.

Having Flaws in Your Camouflage

It makes no sense to spend countless dollars on camouflage if you have a white T-shirt sticking out at the neck or white socks showing. What about your face and hands? Are they hidden with gloves, paints, powders or a mask? Is your gun camo, or at least a flat, dull finish? Anything shiny could alert a bird to your presence. What about glasses? Do you wear metal framed ones? They could cause glare from the sun that spooks a bird.

This hunter is making the mistake of not wearing a face mask. (Credit: Gerald A. Almy)

Take Care in Choosing the Camouflage Itself as Well

Is the pattern you've chosen appropriate for the type of background, vegetation, and topography you're hunting? Take some of the clothing you wear and lay it out in the woods against a tree or have a friend put it on and see if it blends in. If yours doesn't blend in well enough, try another pattern. Choose grays, blacks and browns earlier in the season, ones with some green as leaf-out occurs later in the spring.

Trying to Get Too Close to the Gobbler

It's tempting to want to get as tight to a gobbling bird as possible. You don't want other hens or other hunters to lure him in before you can. And the closer you are, the more fired up he's likely to be. But if you take one step too close, the game is over. Err on the side of caution. Late in the year with thick vegetation, you might be able to get within 80–100 yards. But during early season in open terrain you might have to call from 200 yards or more.

Arriving Too Late

It's hard to believe how early you have to get up to be a successful turkey hunter. If there's a drive involved or much of a hike, it may mean 3 or 4 A.M. You need to be totally in position where you've roosted a bird or expect to hear one calling, cooled down from the hike and listening as the first gray hint of dawn arrives.

Going to the First Bird You Hear

Don't be too hasty. Even though it's vital to be in the woods early, listening, you don't want to rush to the first bird you hear. Wait a bit longer and you may hear two or three more gobblers closer than the first one or in locations that offer a better calling setup. Give any birds nearby a good chance to sound off before you select the best one to try for.

Hiding Too Well

Some hunters feel that a gobbler's eyesight is so good they would do best to hunker way back in a brushpile or overgrown deadfall and wait, totally hidden. That's a mistake. Unless the bird comes in right in front, it makes it harder to see him. It's also difficult to move your gun or turn around if you have to switch your angle for a bird that comes in from a different location than you expected. Simply wear good camouflage and sit with your back against a thick tree trunk at least as wide as your body, when possible. Pull your knees up and prop the gun over the opposite knee. And wait.

Wearing Red, White or Blue Clothing

This is a terrible safety mistake. These are all colors a gobbler can display when it is fired up with the mating urge. An unsafe hunter could mistake you for a bird. Dress in total camouflage and bring some fluorescent orange in your vest that you can wear when walking into or out of the woods after the hunt or moving to a new location.

Not Using a Rangefinder

There may be a few people who can always accurately estimate range in the woods and fields, but most of us can't. Buy a decent rangefinder and use it. Don't whip it out when a bird is coming in. Instead, as soon as you set up in a location, check a couple of nearby landmarks so you know when a gobbler comes near those how far away he will be and whether it's close enough to make the shot.

Calling Too Often

One can never say exactly how much calling is best, but odds are for a hunter of average skills, the mistake is usually too much calling rather than too little. This gives more chance to make mistakes or sound unrealistic, and also may make the tom think, "If she's that fired up, I'll just sit back and let her come to me." After all, that's the way it is done in nature most of the time. It's particularly important not to call too much to a tom while he's still on the roost.

Unimaginative Calling

Just as important as not calling too much is not getting stuck in a rut. Don't use the exact same sequence of calls from the same mouth or box call every time you head out to the woods. Soon the local birds will begin to know you and how to avoid you. Hens don't sound the same every time they talk.

Mix it up with different brands of calls, designs, materials, and the sequences you use. Try cutting mixed in with yelping and clucking. Use aggressive purrs, maybe even a kee-kee run. And mix up the number of yelps you use and their pitch. You

Use a variety of calls—don't get stuck in a rut.
(Credit: Gerald A. Almy)

have to experiment to find out what each individual tom wants, and that may be something entirely different from one day to the next.

Stopping after You Make a Bad Call

This is another common mistake. Hunters freeze up and stop in midcall if a note comes out off-key or squeaky. That just draws attention to the mistake. Simply ignore the bad note and keep the calling sequence going. Real turkeys make some bad sounds now and then, too. But they don't stop and worry about it. They just keep calling.

Using the Wrong Gun

An all-around shotgun or upland bird gun is not what you want for a turkey hunt. The best course of action is to save up and get one of the specially designed guns offered by all manufacturers for this specialized sport. It needs a full or extra-full choke, camouflage or dull finish and should handle 3-inch magnum, 12-gauge or larger shells, although smaller hunters can get by with a 20-gauge by letting birds get closer. A good double sight, tube sight, or scope is vital for accurate aiming in sometimes poor light, and you'll want a sling for the walk in and out of the woods.

Not Being Ready When a Bird Comes In

I've made this mistake more than once, as most veteran turkey hunters have. But you learn from your mistakes, and this one is particularly humiliating and frustrating. To go through all the effort of finding a tom, setting up just right, calling him in and then not being ready with the gun up, aimed and in firing position when it appears is one of the most maddening mistakes you can make.

As soon as you set up, prop your gun over your knees. When a bird starts to approach, lean down into the gun and have it pointing in the direction the tom is coming from. Then only a slight adjustment will be required before you shoot. Make that last final movement when the bird's head goes behind a tree.

Shooting When a Bird is in Strut

A bird in strut has its feathers all puffed out and neck compressed and somewhat hidden. It makes a bad target. Yes, occasionally you'll kill a bird this way. But other times you might simply wound it—a terrible outcome. Make the bird come out of strut by clucking or yelping once or twice, or simply wait until it comes out of strut. The best shot of all is when a bird's neck is outstretched.

Leaving the Woods Too Early

The first hour of dawn is a magical time during turkey season, and it's a great time to bag a bird. But if you don't score, avoid the temptation to quit and leave the woods. Around 8 or 9 or even 10 A.M., lots of hens will have left the gobblers. The toms will again be looking for action and will often be eager to come to your calls. The best hunters know that from about 8:30 A.M. until noon is often a hot time to bag a turkey. Any bird that gobbles then is likely without a hen and a good candidate to call in.

Shooting through Brush

A dense load with hundreds of pellets in it would seem like it could plow through a little brush and a couple of saplings. Don't bet on it. Such cover will deflect the shot and destroy the integrity of the pattern, causing a miss, or worse, a wounded bird. Wait a few minutes and chances are the gobbler will move out of the thickets and into a clearer spot where you can harvest it cleanly.

Giving up Too Easily

If a bird doesn't come right in to your calls, don't give up and head home or go look for other birds. Instead, try switching to another type of call, or try different sequences of calls. Still no luck? Try moving, either parallel, or away from the bird. Don't move towards it or you may spook it, but moving sideways or even away can sometimes stir a bird up and bring him in. He may think you're leaving and not want to let you get away. Also try simply not calling, but waiting silently. This can sometimes pique his curiosity and bring him in.

Not Learning from Mistakes!

This is the single biggest mistake of all that you can make. If you don't analyze your hunts—the good and the bad—you're not improving as a turkey hunter and could well make the same mistakes again next time in the woods.

The Teachings of Don Pepé

By Thomas McIntyre

When Mito broke trail he raised the machete as if lifting his hat above his head, then let the blade fall, the force of its weight and velocity shearing the vines and branches. It looked perfectly smooth and effortless, the steel ringing like a chime—announcing to me I was hunting Mexico again.

There are easier lands to hunt than Mexico. The bureaucracy can be Kafkaesque; travel difficult and risky; virulent illness in the next sip of water. Set beside that, though, is the fact that there are things to be seen in Mexico that can be seen nowhere else. And that one can come to love hunting there.

The machete's chime reminded me of that, and also of the last note of the "song" of one of those things to be seen only in Mexico, the ocellated turkey, the rest of whose spring mating

199

call defied imitation or comparison: prepared pianos, perhaps, combined with large atonal arboreal amphibians. Once heard, though, it was remembered, even if, like some secret oath, it could not be repeated to anyone else.

The ocellated is the second of the world's two species of wild turkeys. The other is the unfortunately named "common" turkey known throughout North America, including Mexico.

A. Starker Leopold in his *Wildlife of Mexico* called the ocellated turkey, found on the Yucatán Peninsula, "one of the finest game-birds of Mexico," feeling compelled to add, "and for that matter, of North America." The first time I saw one, I had to agree.

In a private menagerie on a large hacienda outside Mérida, Yucatán, a beardless gobbler trotted back and forth in his wire-caged pen. His breast and back feathers were coppery, wings brown, white, iridescent green, and barred black-and-white. Gray tail feathers were spotted with peacock "eyes," or *ocelli*; his needle spurs longer than the rays on a vaquero's silver rowels. Oddest was a knobbed head of naked turquoise skin, covered with glowing orange wartlike carbuncles. Hell, this could be the finest gamebird in the *world*; and I immediately knew I had to hunt one.

I also knew where I would go to hunt this most Mexican jungle fowl, this plumed hallucination, and with whom I would hunt him. It could only be in Campeche state, and with my old friend, Don Pepé.

I'd first gotten to know Don Pepé some years earlier on the road to ruins. Before light we had left his Snook Inn hotel along the Champoton River, heading toward the Mayan ruins at Edzná, bound for a maize field to hunt white-winged doves and red-billed pigeons.

Fog was in the winter air; and as the sky turned apricot through the window of the old VW van, Don Pepé, sitting beside me on the bench seat in the back, declared, "This is something in which I disagree with Shakespeare.

"'Tis the very witching time of the night,' does not Hamlet say at midnight?" continued Don Pepé, waving toward the dawning sky. "But *this*, I think, is the true witching time."

The outline of Don Pepé's life owes much to the bewitched vagaries of twentieth century history. His birth in Vera Cruz had been eventuated by a series of turns that began with the diversion of the ship his mother and grandmother had been sailing from Europe to Buenos Aires at the outbreak of World War I, and their subsequent separation from the rest of their family until the Armistice. Married five times himself, and father of ten, Don Pepé (more formally, Señor José Sansores) has been quoting Shakespeare, Churchill, and similar luminaries for over fifty years while guiding and outfitting in the jungle, the *selva*, of Campeche. In the past he went after jaguar (hunting them with shotguns and buckshot from hammocks suspended above tethered goats), puma, and ocelot; today, peccary, brocket deer, doves, pigeons, ducks, snook, and his favorite, his "children," tarpon. The ocellated turkey, though, remains his most sought-after game.

That first time I hunted with Don Pepé, we remained in the open maize field, trying to hit the deceptively slow-sculling and large wild pigeons and definitely missing the tumbling and yawing whitewings. It is the selva, though, that Don Pepé has always loved, especially as a place to walk and to find coolness in the heat of the day, which in late April comes soon after sunrise.

If Mito, one of Don Pepé's guides, and I, listening at the edges of fields, had heard no singing by the time the sun was up, we would move into the shadows of the selva ourselves. Following trails and washed out roads, sometimes having to cut a way with the machete, we would try to jump an ocellated turkey or search for the coin-sized tracks (*pecas*) of brocket deer, for which I also had a permit, and often find instead the larger tracks of peccary and whitetails.

On the selva floor we would see partridge-like tinamous, said to express a rather liberal view of family values by mating in threes. In the trees would be toucans, crested guan, parrots, woodpeckers, and motmots—"clockbirds" who strip the filaments from the shaft almost to the tip of their central tail feather, then swing it like a pendulum as they perch. Far to the south in tall *ramon* trees we even saw the same "little men" a band of Kiowa reported seeing after traveling deep into Mexico long ago: male howler monkeys.

And once we did see an ocellated gobbler, already in flight through the trees.

Finally, one morning at dawn on a falling down hacienda called Quisil, we heard a gobbler singing in a hilly hardwood thicket across a cut and blackened cane field. Calling is rarely used by Mexicans for ocellated turkey; the hen's call a soft whistle that carries only a very short distance. Instead, the traditional method in Mexico for hunting ocellated turkey is to stalk them.

Mito and I crossed the field, dew holding down the black ash, and crept through the vines and thorns, sweat soaking into my camo. It was a small thicket, but it seemed to take forever to move silently through it as the gobbler sang. Then Mito froze, moving one finger toward a tree.

I stared for several seconds before I saw a dark shape in the limbs. I slowly raised the 12-gauge, then waited.

The *macho*'s knobbed head lifted, and he looked around. Then he flapped to the ground. The brush was not very thick here, but the bird would be gone in an instant. I moved the muzzle to cover his head and neck, take the gun off safe, and squeeze the trigger.

Wings beat on the ground as Mito sprinted forward, slipping like smoke through the thorns that ripped and tugged at me as I followed. When I reached him, Mito had the bird, and all I could do was stare at something as strange and beautiful as I had ever seen in the wild.

Mito placed the turkey in the burlap bag he carried, and we made the long hike back to the van where Don Pepé's eldest son, Jorge, waited, reading a paperback Western, written in Spanish. When we met up with Don Pepé that morning, he smiled with some pride at the gobbler and said, "This is the gift we give our friends."

The world's-record ocellated weighs only 12-1/2 pounds with spurs just over 2 inches. My gobbler was an ounce or two under 11½ pounds with 1⅜-inch spurs. Rather than determining if he qualified for record classification, though, we did something far more appropriate, skinning him and letting Don Pepé's chefs turn him into an exquisite *mole con pavo ocelado*.

On the drive back to Mérida Don Pepé, dressed in a white guayabera and with gaunt-shanked old-man's legs sticking out of Bermudas, took the wheel of the van. His fifth wife, wearing a hearing-aid bought out of an outdoor catalog (intended to enhance hunters' ears), reached over from the back to feed him cold peeled wedges of the sapodilla tree's persimmony *zapote* fruit. As he drove he told me of his inventions he never patented (adjustable wipers, "heads-up" aircraft instrumentation); the woodscraft he had learned (such as his conviction that yellow hammocks repel insects because they are the color of fire, which, of course, all animal life abhors); his acquaintance with space-flight *meister*mind Wernher von Braun; how *El Diablo* himself got the drop on him one night in a jungle hut when Pepé could not get to his pistol; and how some people share a "radio channel" in their heads over which unique ideas and insights may be transmitted simultaneously. Glancing at an overpass and seeing laughing boys holding a 4-foot iguana aloft, as if to hurl it down on us, I realized that in Mexico "magic realism" was not merely a literary genre. You only had to look at the ocellated turkey to see that.

In the city I shook hands with Don Pepé outside a small hotel built around a fountain. He handed me a box with the skinned and salted pelt of my wild turkey, and we bid each other, *"Hasta luego."* Placing my trophy in my room, I then went in frantic search of store-bought souvenirs before my morning flight. I found something for my wife quickly, but it was more difficult for my five-year-old. In a hardware store window, though, I saw exactly what I was looking for.

Though not as large as the one Mito wielded, it is much too big for my son now, so I have put it away in its tooled leather sheath on a high shelf in the closet, where it rests beside a Zulu *assegai* and an Tibetan dagger. The edge is good, though, and the steel rings just like a chime when struck. Maybe by the time he grows into it my son will be ready to hunt Mexico with me, and perhaps with Don Pepé, too, to see what can be seen nowhere else on earth.

Christmas Turkey

By John McDaniel

The phone's insistent ringing interrupted the Christmas Eve news broadcast. I picked up the receiver and was about to say hello when Jack's intense voice cut me off. "I found them! I got into the flock! There must have been ten! I scattered them near Saunder's property line!"

Shocked, I managed a profound, "What!"

Jack's eager voice rose a note as he added information to his explanation. "I scattered the big flock on George's place at sunset. Let's go after them in the morning!"

Understanding the situation now, I asked if Jack was confident that the turkeys had flushed in several directions. He replied, impatiently, that the birds had scattered. "Let's go!" Jack repeated, adding, "You know Nelle won't mind." I turned toward my wife, Jack's sister, and tried to briefly explain the situation.

Nelle listened and then said "Oh good, a Christmas turkey!" We both smiled at her optimism and I turned back to the phone to arrange a Christmas morning rendezvous with Jack. Thoughts of turkeys and the enjoyable task of preparing for a hunt comprised a pleasant disruption to the remaining hours of Christmas Eve.

Only the most indulgent of parents were awake with their children when I stepped into the still, cold, darkness of Christmas morning. After a quick breakfast, I gathered my equipment and sat on the dark porch enjoying the deserted street as I waited for Jack. I heard the Jeep a block away as it rattled through the quiet town of Lexington, Virginia. Soon I sat in the front seat, cramped by the heavy clothes, guns, and accessories. We talked of Jack's encounter with the turkey and our chances for success as we drove out of the town and into the hills.

During the fall and winter season we have learned the one time we have a fair chance of taking this great gamebird is after a flock has been scattered. The young turkey's gregarious tendencies offset his intelligence and great senses of sight and hearing, making him susceptible to the hunter who has learned to imitate his lost call. In his eagerness to relocate other members of the flock, the young turkeys will often come rapidly to a call, and can occasionally be deceived by only a fair imitation of his voice.

With respect to calls in general, we have found that the whistling kee-kee of the young turkey is by far the most reliable. The young birds will come to lost calls produced on any type of caller. But we have enjoyed particularly impressive success with the kee-kee calls made on a mouth-operated yelper of the Turpin variety. Regardless of the caller, it is important that the hunter locate the precise spot from which the turkeys flushed when scattered. If dispersed, the turkeys will regroup at, or very close to, the spot from which they scattered. The speed with which they return to the scatter point will depend on a number of factors, including the time of the day, the nature of the threat that scattered them, and the ages of the birds comprising the flock. Turkeys scattered early in the day will usually regroup with some speed, often beginning to call shortly after the hunter has concealed himself. Birds scattered later in the day will often wait until late in the evening before regrouping. A flock that is split up right before sunset will make an effort to re-group just after dawn the next morning.

If the birds are scattered and pursued, by dogs for example, the process of regrouping may be delayed for days as the fright-ened and widely dispersed birds will have problems locating each other. A flock consisting of younger birds, and conse-quently those who are less likely to have encountered deception, will regroup more rapidly. Under normal circumstances, a flock scattered by a single hunter's shots will regroup at the scatter-point. The one major threat to this strategy is the failure to effec-tively scatter the birds. Poor dispersion of the birds will mean they will reunite soon after landing in close proximity to one an-other with no need to return to the spot where they flushed.

It is important for the hunter to locate the precise spot from which the turkeys flush when scattered. (Credit: John McDaniel)

Climbing a Ridge is Hard Work

By the time Jack had finished a detailed account of the previous afternoon's hunt, the Jeep had left the hard surface road and was climbing an old logging trail. After several rough moments the Jeep lurched to a stop and we climbed out onto the cold mountain. I quickly secured my equipment and followed Jack up the ridge. The climb was steep and we were both breathless when Jack stopped, turned and said, "That's where they flushed, right by the big pine over there." Jack said he would go to the north side of the ridge; I decided to stay as close as possible to the spot where the birds had scattered.

We parted and I began to look for a suitable place to call from. I selected a clump of laurel that surrounded the base of a large oak. I eased myself into the laurel and modified the natural

The author calls from behind a natural blind of laurel at the base of a large oak. (Credit: John McDaniel)

blind by clearing a small area so I could move slightly without disturbing the vegetation. Satisfied with the concealment that the location afforded, I pulled out my turkey call, shells, and camouflage nets for both my face and hands from the small day pack in which I also carry my lunch and a few emergency items.

Light filtered slowly over the eastern ridges and I enjoyed the beauty of dawn mixed with the anticipation of turkeys. I was confident I would hear turkeys calling. But the first sounds were not turkeys but roosters in the valley far below. A few moments later the raucous call of crows came from higher on the ridge. Light enough now to read the labels on my shotgun shells, I checked the number six on the big 3-inch hulls and placed them in the chambers of my gun. I closed it quietly and gently placed the shotgun on the ground, pulled the head net over my face, put on the gloves, picked up the call, and waited.

The first call was distant but clear. As I had anticipated, it was the whistling kee-kee run of the young turkey. I put the yelper to my mouth, tightened my throat and listened with some satisfaction as I produced a fair imitation of the kee-kee whistle I had just heard. The turkey answered immediately. I responded with another call, trying to interject the pleading anxiety implicit in the bird's call. Again the turkey answered my call. I waited until the bird's long series of whistling notes ceased and then, immediately, prepared to call again.

I never worry about calling too much when working with scattered young turkeys in the fall and winter. I have found that the turkey will often become suspicious if one calls sparingly. In the spring season, frequent calls may be disadvantageous but in the fall and winter the lost turkey expects other members of the flock to respond readily, and it will be to the hunter's advantage to answer every call a bird makes.

Before I finished my next series the bird initiated its response and the ringing call was perceptibly closer. The call was so much closer that I was confident I could calculate, with some precision, where the bird would appear. I focused my attention on a clump of laurel which was directly in front of the spot from which the bird last called. I waited straining for any sound which would indicate the turkey's progress toward the blind. After several moments of intense waiting, the turkey's call rang out again, this time it came directly from the clump of laurel. My left hand went down to the shotgun and I brought it up, the rib of the gun moving up slowly into my field of vision. With the gun bearing on the laurel, I waited for the bird to materialize. Seconds passed and the shotgun's weight began to take its toll and my body trembled. I strained to see into the laurel and to hear movement in the leaves. Suddenly the bird clucked, a soft questioning note, which I recognized as a demand for reassurance. Awkwardly I altered my position, reached for the call, and put it to my mouth once again. I prepared my mouth and throat for the new call and directed a soft cluck toward the laurel and the hidden, but close, turkey. The bird responded, immediately, with another cluck. A conversation in clucks followed. Despite his willingness to converse, the turkey refused to move.

Frustration set in as I extended the conversation with the stationary bird. Finally, impatient with the stalemate, I tried another loud kee-kee call and incredibly, another turkey answered from my rear! This bird did not sound as if it were over 100 yards away and I was perplexed. Should I turn? I decided to remain facing the first turkey. Not knowing which way to direct my call, I made another kee-kee whistle. The newcomer answered immediately and I perceived a sense of urgency in his high-pitched voice. Before I could respond, he called again and the terminating yelps were clear and significantly closer. I twisted my contorted body in a commitment to the newcomer and brought the suddenly heavy and awkward shotgun into position. The turkey's next call came from behind a screen offered

by a fallen tree some 40 yards from my position. "Young gobbler," I thought as I caught the distinctly coarse yelps at the end
of his call. My heart began to race as I heard the sound of his
feet in the leaves as he came closer.

A flash of black behind a screen of laurel was my first visible
evidence of his presence. His body quickly materialized as he
came at a rapid but dignified walk. His eagerness to find the
other turkey was obvious but there was also a controlled suspi-
cion in his manner. He stopped suddenly, the lower portion of
his body hidden behind a log. I brought the shotgun to bear.
The turkey's proud head was stationary; one searching eye large
and bright. I balanced the head on the silver bead and pressed
the trigger. The harsh recoil jarred me and distorted my vision.
When my eyes refocused, the turkey's head had been replaced
by his graceful tail, which was fanned up in the air and quiver-
ing gently. I jumped awkwardly from my blind and yelled with
joy aware that the vibrating tail was indicative of an immobile
and mortally wounded bird. Despite my conviction that he was
immobilized, I quickly ran to him.

I looked down at my turkey with awe. There was a frozen
power in his immense and powerful legs and feet, the large,
clear eyes, the broad and graceful wings, the solid body and the
feathers gleaming black, brown, and bronze in the sun. I was
pleased that the No. 6 shot had torn into the unfeathered portion of his neck and killed him instantly. After admiring the
bird for several seconds, I picked him up and carried him back
to my blind. The distance was a short 21 paces. Twenty-one
paces is about right. Forget your 50- and 60-yard shotguns. I am
convinced that with any shotgun, more turkeys will escape
than will be killed at 40 yards, let alone 50. I say 35 yards is
maximum and 25 is better.

Sitting by my blind with my turkey, I tried to open my small
knapsack to get a snack. I smiled to myself as I acknowledged

the fact that my hands were shaking. I enjoyed the quiet pause before the proud walk down the mountain. The turkey had been taken fairly and killed cleanly. I experienced a relaxed warmth. I ate the cold goose sandwich slowly, relishing the satisfaction of the moment. Finally, I packed everything neatly away, picked up the turkey by his feet, swung him over my shoulder, and headed down the slope.

A turkey is heavy but not too heavy. Unlike other prestigious forms of game, a turkey can be carried proudly by the man who killed it. Jack smiled when he saw the turkey. As I took it off my shoulder, he said, "Thank goodness! When I heard you yell I was afraid you'd shot your foot off!" I laughed, and we both turned our attention to the great bird. We admired the turkey together, and Jack listened attentively as I described the kill.

It was after 9 A.M. when the Jeep entered town. Jack parked the vehicle in front of my dogs' kennels and three confused Brittanies watched with interest as I sprinted into the house with our Christmas turkey.

Index